TOEFL/TOEIC Express

Grammaire

Florent GUSDORF

ellipses

Dans la série *Bloc-notes* anglais

- ***Express yourself!*** *15 chapitres thématiques pour connaître l'essentiel du vocabulaire courant en anglais* [niveau 1]
- ***Check in.*** *Communiquer efficacement en anglais* [niveau 2]
- ***Help!*** *Grammaire et vocabulaire de base en anglais,* 2e éd. [niveau 1]
- ***Fifty-Fifty.*** *Réviser son vocabulaire anglais en s'amusant* [Spécial sciences]
- ***English: why not?*** *Les bases de l'anglais* [niveau A1]
- ***XPression.*** *Plus de 1300 expressions idiomatiques de l'anglais d'aujourd'hui* [niveau 2]

du même auteur

- ***English Academy*** *Les 50 fautes d'usage les plus fréquentes en anglais* [niveau 2]
- ***Key Words English.*** *Vocabulaire de la vie de tous les jours* [niveau 2]
- ***Complete to compete.*** *Réviser son vocabulaire anglais, thèmes de société* [niveau 2]
- ***TOEFL/TOEIC Express.*** *Vocabulaire, auto-évaluation* [niveau 2]

Pour les autres langues,
retrouvez les titres disponibles de la série *Bloc-notes*
à la fin de cet ouvrage.

ISBN 978-2-7298-4292-5

www.editions-ellipses.fr

PREFACE

TOEFL/TOEIC EXPRESS **Grammaire** est destiné à tous ceux qui se préparent aux examens internationaux en anglais et souhaitent faire une vérification rapide de leurs connaissances grammaticales.

TOEFL/TOEIC EXPRESS **Grammaire** comprend 97 chapitres couvrant les principaux points de la grammaire qu'il convient de maîtriser pour aborder sereinement les épreuves. Deux tableaux (verbes irréguliers et *phrasal verbs* complètent l'ouvrage).

TOEFL/TOEIC EXPRESS **Grammaire** propose une gamme variée de 245 exercices : repérage des erreurs, QCM, exercices de clausure, exercices de logique. Figurent également de courts textes et des exercices de ré-écriture ou de traduction. Les exercices sont intégralement corrigés, voire annotés, et permettent ainsi à l'étudiant de vérifier ses réponses.

TOEFL/TOEIC EXPRESS **Grammaire** ne vise pas à l'exhaustivité. Néanmoins, il permettra à l'étudiant de faire une mise au point des domaines qu'il faut maîtriser avant d'aborder avec lucidité et confiance les tests d'expression et de compréhension écrite et orale.

TOEFL/TOEIC EXPRESS **Grammaire** est le complément indispensable à ***TOEFL/TOEIC EXPRESS*** **Vocabulaire** paru chez le même éditeur (2008).

CONTENTS

1 QUESTION TAGS (1)

1. Express *surprise* using tags.

1. He was admitted to Stanford at the age of 15. ....
2. He speaks several languages fluently. ....
3. He used to be a bit of a ladies' man when he was young. ....
4. I've got too much work to do and can't go out with you. ....
5. The President has just dissolved Parliament. ....
6. He must be operated on straight away. ....

2. Express *sarcasm* using tags.

1. He has just bought a Maserati. ....
2. He will be climbing 3 K8 this summer. ....
3. He would have loved to go sailing. ....
4. His parents have rented a yacht for the holidays. ....

3. Express *agreement* using tags.

1. The sea has got choppy! .... **2**. The rifle was loaded. .... **3**. The hotel prices were outrageous. .... **4**. We used to be happy. .... **5**. We might be delayed, the traffic is heavy. ....

4. Express *disagreement* using tags.

1. Have you lost the office keys? No, ...
2. She will forget to give us a call. No, ...
3. I suppose I must dress up for the cocktail party. No, ...
4. I was here long before you were. No, ...

5. Express *disagreement* with negative statements using tags.

1. He can't have missed his flight. No, ...
2. "You never forget anything." "No, ..."
3. The blue whale won't become extinct. No, ...
4. Not all states have restored the death penalty in the USA. No, ...

6. Express *confirmation* using tags.

1. "She's rather clever." "Yes ...." **2**. "She's got green eyes." "Yes ...." **3**. "You'll have to try again." "Yes ...." **4**. "John's in a good mood this morning." "Yes ...." **5**. "We're in for another storm." "Yes ...."

Correction

1. **1**. Was he? - **2**. Does he? - **3**. Did he? - **4**. Have you? - **5**. He can't have - **6**. Must he?

2. **1**. Oh, he has, has he? **2**. Oh, he will, will he? **3**. Oh, he would, would he? **4**. Oh, they have, have they?

3. **1**. Yes, it has, hasn't it? **2**. Yes, it was, wasn't it? **3**. Yes, they were, weren't they? **4**. Yes, we were, weren't we? **5**. Yes, we might, mightn't we?

4. **1**. No, I haven't. **2**. No, she won't. **3**. No, you needn't. **4**. No, you weren't.

5. **1**. No, he can't have. **2**. No, I don't. **3**. No, it won't. **4**. No, they haven't.

6. **1**. Yes she is, isn't she? **2**. Yes she has, hasn't she? **3**. Yes I will, won't I? **4**. Yes he is, isn't he? **5**. Yes we are, aren't we?

2 QUESTION TAGS (2)

1. Use elements in brackets to compare statements.

1. Acid rock gets on my nerves. (rap music) So ....
2. Strawberries are in season. (raspberries) So ....
3. Recruits must do as they are told. (you) So ....
4. He needed help with his math. (brother) So ....
5. You seemed to be having a good time last night. (your fiancé)
So ....
6. Immigrants have to work hard to succeed. (we all)
So ....

2. Use elements in brackets to express difference.

1. When I am on holiday, I don't get up very early. (the rest of the family) ....
2. The first rocket didn't start. (the spare one) ....
3. California doesn't get much rain. (Arizona) ....
4. I needn't leave early. (You) ....
5. He dared not jump from the pier. (his sister) ....
6. His father couldn't come. (mother) ....
7. He had never had his eyes tested. (ears) ....
8. He hadn't had a decent meal in two years. (drink) ....

3. Express affirmation or negation of statements (*I do / I don't*).

1. He never makes mistakes. ....
2. He never used to make mistakes. ....
3. He won't give you the answer. ....
4. You'll need a visa. ....
5. She doesn't like broccoli. ....

4. Complete the sentences.

1. "Can you tell his friends he's moved to Cuba?" "Don't worry, I ...." **2**. "Can you give a hand with my math?" "I'm sorry. I .... if I .... but I ...." **3**. If the bank won't lend you any money, your dad .... **4**. The president said he wouldn't sign the bill and indeed he .... **5**. She told me she'd call once a week and she .... **6**. "Isn't she on a strict diet?" "She .... but she no longer is."

Correction

1. **1**. So does rap music. **2**. So are raspberries. **3**. So must you. **4**. So did his brother. **5**. So did your fiancé. **6**. So do we all.

2. **1**. Neither do the rest of the family / The rest of the family don't either. **2**. The spare one didn't either / Neither did the spare one. **3**. Neither does Arizona / Arizona doesn't either. **4**. You don't have to either. **5**. Neither did his sister. **6**. Neither could his mother / His mother couldn't either. **7**. Or his ears either / Nor had he had his ears tested / He hadn't had his ears tested either. **8**. Nor a decent drink / He hadn't had a decent drink either.

3. **1**. I do. **2**. I did. **3**. I will. **4**. I won't. **5**. I do.

4. **1**. will - **2**. would / could / can't - **3**. will - **4**. didn't - **5**. did - **6**. used to be

3 INVERSION (1)

Circle the letter of the correct answer.

1. ... great was the destruction that the South took decades to recover.
a) Very b) Too c) So d) Such

2. The crash might never have occurred ... the two trains been on schedule.
a) if b) had c) unless d) were

3. The Minister had no sooner arrived ... the meeting started.
a) as b) than c) that d) for

4. ... are the juice and pulp of the grape useful, but various products are made from the skin and seeds.
a) Not that they b) Neither c) They never d) Not only

5. Throughout Maine ... summer music camps, where young people and adults may study.
a) is where b) located are c) to be found d) there are

6. On few occasions ... a film so much.
a) I am enjoying b) did I enjoy c) have I enjoyed d) I was enjoyed

7. Never ... been so many people in such a tiny place.
a) have there b) they have c) has it d) there have

8. Union leaders now understand that ... must if they want the plant to remain open.
a) they negotiate b) negotiate them
c) negotiate they d) them negotiate

9. Only after sanctions had been taken ... agree to enforce international laws.
a) they b) they did c) were they d) did they

10. ... to Central Park last night, I would have heard Elton John sing in the rain.
a) Had I gone b) If I went
c) Should I go d) If I were to go

11. ... you see Clive, ask him to ring me tonight.
a) Do b) Will c) ø d) Should

12. Never at any time ... that he was allergic to shellfish.
a) said he b) had he said
c) he said d) he had said

13. No sooner had the bride arrived ... the ceremony started.
a) when b) that c) than d) ø

14. ... did they know that the police had them under surveillance.
a) Much b) Few c) Many d) Little

15. ... convincing was he that we were all taken in.
a) So b) Such
c) He was such d) As

Correction

1c - 2b - 3b - 4d - 5d - 6c - 7a - 8c - 9d - 10a - 11d - 12b -13c - 14d - 15a

4 INVERSION (2)

1. Circle the mistakes and correct them. Write R for Right.

1. R / W............... Did the dog not bark, he would never have heard that somebody was trying to break into the house.

2. R / W............... Did you find my old school reports, bring them back, would you?

3. R / W............... Was a serious incident take place, the people living next to the nuclear power plant would be evacuated.

4. R / W............... Not until 1865 Joseph Lister tried the first antiseptic treatment on a compound fracture.

5. R / W............... You simply must come to my show, and so do they.

6. R / W............... At no time my husband told me of his decision to look for a new job.

2. Write sentences using words in brackets.

1. There had been the greatest famine Ireland had ever experienced. (NEVER BEFORE)

....

2. Olivia had just closed the door when the telephone rang. (NO SOONER)

....

3. Demy had never thought that she would win the prize. (LITTLE)

....

4. I had rarely enjoyed reading a thriller so much. (SELDOM)

....

3. Combine the numbered elements with the lettered ones.

1. They never go out to the cinema	**a.** has any region sustained such rapid growth for so long.
2. Little had the mountaineers	**b.** must you leave your luggage unattended.
3. Hardly had the company been taken over	**c.** nor do they go to the theatre.
4. Little did the young novelist	**d.** when his career took off.
5. Never before in world history	**e.** when he took to his heels.
6. Hardly had the thief seen me	**f.** think he would be awarded the Booker Prize.
7. On very few occasions	**g.** expected they would be trapped so close to the summit.
8. Under no circumstances	**h.** have I enjoyed a play so much.

Correction

1. **1**. Had the dog not barked - **2**. Should you find - **3**. Were a serious incident to take place - **4**. did JL try - **5**. so must they - **6**. At no time did my husband tell me.

2. **1**. Never before had Ireland experienced such a great famine. **2**. No sooner had Olivia closed the door than the telephone rang. **3**. Little had Demy thought she would win the prize. **4**. Seldom had I enjoyed reading a thriller so much.

3. 1c - 2g - 3d - 4f - 5a - 6e - 7h - 8b

5 HAVE

1. Complete the sentences using *have* expressions. Put *have* in the correct form.

have bacon • have this dream • have fun / a ball • have a holiday • have a look • have a meeting • have the opportunity • have a party • have a rest • have a shower

1. I .... at the house tomorrow and if I like it, I'll have my wife come down and see it.
2. He was so tired when he came back that he just lay down. As far as I know, he's still in his room ....
3. He came back from his cricket game, ... and left. He told me he was going to a .... that the neighbors .... tonight.
4. Let's .... tomorrow to discuss the new contract.
5. When she was young, she .... to go and work in Australia. But then she got married and chose to stay in Germany with her family.
6. He's a workaholic. He (not) .... for several years.
7. Most British people .... and eggs for breakfast.
8. "Did you enjoy yourself at Sarah's party?" "Oh yes, we ...."
9. When she was a teenager, she .... of becoming a model.

2. Complete the sentences using the correct form of *have*.

1. He .... a new book published this month. **2**. I .... a party next week. Would you like to come? **3**. We .... a new kitchen for a week. Wanna come and see it? **4**. I .... go now or I'll be late for my first class. **5**. At what time (you) .... lunch? **6**. Why (you) .... pay so much tax? **7**. You (not) .... time to catch your flight even if you had hurried. **8**. You (not) .... believe what she tells you. **9**. You (not) .... go. There's a storm warning out. **10**. (You) .... your eyes examined? **11**. You .... be back by 10 o'clock. **12**. (You) .... to attend mass every Sunday? **13**. I .... a new computer than my brother's crappy one.

3. Spot the mistakes and correct them. Write R for Right.

1. R / W............... As tragedy had it, both were killed in a car accident earlier this year.
2. R / W............... "Why have you to carry so much luggage when you travel?"
3. R / W............... How often have you have your oil checked?
4. R / W............... Have you a light?
5. R / W............... You have not to apologize. I'm to blame.

Correction

1. **1**. 'll have a look - **2**. having a rest - **3**. had a shower / party / are having - **4**. have a meeting - **5**. had the opportunity - **6**. hasn't had a holiday - **7**. have bacon - **8**. had fun - **9**. had a dream

2. **1**. is having - **2**. 'm having - **3**. have had - **4**. had better - **5**. do you have - **6**. do you have to - **7**. wouldn't have had - **8**. don't have to - **9**. had better not / 'd better not - **10**. Did you have - **11**. have got to - **12**. Did you have to - **13**. I'd rather have

3. **1**. R - **2**. Why do you have to carry - **3**. do you have your oil checked - **4**. Do you have a light - **5**. You don't have to apologize

6 SIMPLE / CONTINUOUS FORM (1)

1. Spot the possible mistakes and correct them. Write R for Right.

1. R / W............... I'm understanding that the contract will not be signed as expected.
2. R / W............... I'm thinking I'll buy a new computer.
3. R / W............... The table is measuring 3 ft.
4. R / W............... This book contains the results of years of research.
5. R / W............... They're owning a big yacht and a villa on the Riviera.
6. R / W............... Stop waffling. You're being silly.
7. R / W............... Are you hearing the music next door?
8. R / W............... Two fierce mastiffs were smelling the bone.
9. R / W............... The music they're playing is sounding like Puccini.
10. R / W............... I'm not sure I'm agreeing with you.
11. R / W............... He was losing and was hating it by the minute.
12. R / W............... I've been knowing the Martins for years.

2. Choose the correct sentence. Circle the letter of the correct answer.

1. **(a)** They can see **(b)** They are seeing the sea from their house.
2. **(a)** The referee is blowing his whistle. **(b)** The referee blows his whistle. We've lost again.
3. **(a)** What does Jane do? **(b)** What is Jane doing?
4. **(a)** She watches TV every evening. **(b)** She's watching TV every evening.
5. **(a)** She's resembling her mother. **(b)** She resembles her mother.
6. **(a)** He always gets tied up in knots with Molly. **(b)** He's getting tied up in knots with Molly.

3. Circle the letter of the correct answer.

1. The city lies on the coast *refers to*
a) permanent position b) temporary position
2. People were lying on the beach *refers to*
a) permanent position b) temporary position
3. The statue stands in the main square *refers to*
a) permanent position b) temporary position
4. She was standing over me, looking at what I was writing *refers to*
a) permanent position b) temporary position
5. Our new neighbors are being friendly *suggests*
a) they are friendly b) their friendliness may not last

Correction

1. **1**. I understand (verb of opinion) - **2**. think but I'm thinking of buying a computer - **3**. measure (static) - **4**. R - **5**. own (possession) - **6**. R - **7**. Can you hear (perception) - **8**. a bone smells or a dog smells a bone - **9**. sounds (verb of appearance, like seem, look, appear) - **10**. agree - **11**. R ; action in progress - **12**. I've known.

2. **1a** ; can + verbs of perception ; ÷ they are seeing a doctor: *ils voient / ils consultent un médecin.* - **2a** ; action in progress, ; simple present = short action - **3a/b** ; a = what's her job ÷ b = action in progress - **4a** ; habit - **5b** ; description - **6a**

3. 1a - 2b - 3a - 4b - 5b

7 SIMPLE / CONTINUOUS FORM (2)

1. Circle the correct answer.

1. After his match, he was tired / was being tired but happy.
2. She knows / is knowing a lot of good recipes.
3. The soup tastes / is tasting good. Have some.
4. I taste / am tasting the soup to see if it needs more salt.
5. I remember / am remembering you. I saw you at the orals last year.
6. Hi! Mmmm. Something smells / is smelling good. What's cooking / cooks?
7. Julie studies / is studying in France this year.
8. Stress is causing / causes high blood pressure.
9. "What does she do / is she doing?" - "She's a corporate lawyer."
10. Are you getting / Do you get ready for school? It's almost 8, you know.

2. Circle the mistakes in the underlined verbal forms.

1. What will you have? I'm having the fish. I'm being allergic to red meat.
2. My father usually drives me to school but today I walk.
3. Gloria usually is exercising before work but today she's resting.
4. A storm brews. It is windy and rainy. The sky looks overcast.
5. Are you taking a German class this term? Yes, I do.
6. The baby's looking so big. How much does it weigh?
7. He tries to come to class on time because it is starting at 8 sharp.
8. I'm hearing something outside. Are you sure the doors are locked?
9. Mary is hating cooking. So we always eat out.
10. Something is smelling nice here. Are you wearing a new cologne?

3. Circle the correct answer (past simple / continuous).

1. The policeman asked him what he did / was doing at three o'clock.
2. She broke her leg while she skied / she was skiing.
3. Sorry, I wasn't paying attention when you were talking / talked.
4. They drove / were driving too fast when they crashed.
5. Did people wear / Were people wearing jeans 50 years ago?
6. Last week the class was studying / studied a poem by Robert Frost.
7. I didn't know / wasn't knowing your home address so I sent the parcel to your office.
8. In 2008, Roger Federer was winning / won his fifth consecutive U.S. Open title, beating Andy Murray.
9. He was talking on his mobile phone while he drove / was driving his car.
10. Johnny left class early because he was having / had a toothache.

Correction

1. **1**. was tired - **2**. knows - **3**. tastes - **4**. am tasting - **5**. remember - **6**. smells / 's cooking - **7**. is studying - **8**. causes - **9**. does she do - **10**. Are you getting

2. **1**. I'm allergic - **2**. I'm walking - **3**. exercises (habit with usually) - **4**. is brewing (action in progress) - **5**. Yes, I am (ellipsis for are you taking) - **6**. looks (no -ING form) - **7**. starts (habit) - **8**. I can hear (perception, no -ING form) - **9**. hates cooking (no -ING form) - **10**. smells (note : the dog is smelling a bone / you smell nice)

3. **1**. was doing - **2**. was skiing - **3**. were talking - **4**. were driving - **5**. Did people wear - **6**. studied - **7**. didn't know - **8**. won - **9**. was driving - **10**. had

8 PRESENT SIMPLE / CONTINUOUS (1)

1. Spot the possible mistakes and correct them. Write R for Right.

	Correction
1. I'm born in Belfast.	
2. It is often raining in Scotland.	
3. They go to Venice for their honeymoon.	
4. He always complains about his neighbor every time we see him.	
5. He teaches German in a New England college.	
6. I'm reading *The Economist* every week.	
7. I feel hungry. Shall we eat now?	
8. I feel we ought to go now.	
9. "What are you up to at this time of night?" "I'm just getting a drink of water, that's all."	
10. He's seeming ill at ease.	
11. You look surprised.	
12. I'm liking traveling.	

2. Put the verbs in brackets in the present simple or continuous.

1. Where's Colin? He's in his room. He probably (watch) .... television. He always (lie) .... on his bed gawping at that thing.

2. Mum (cook) .... some food in the kitchen at the moment. She usually (cook) .... in the mornings.

3. "Where you (go) .... tonight?" "It (be) .... none of your business but since you (ask) .... , if you must know, we (go) .... to a lecture on how to deal with nosey people."

4. I (see) .... you (wear) .... your best clothes. You (go) .... to a party? No, I (go) .... to my sister's wedding. She (get married) .... for the third time.

5. Listen! Our neighbor (play) .... the cello. I (like / not) .... classical music, but I must say it (sound) .... beautiful.

6. You (work) .... here? You (come) .... by bus or you (take) .... the subway? At what time you (leave) .... tonight?

7. The firm (want) .... to slim down the workforce. They (plan) .... to lay off 7,000 workers.

Correction

1. **1**. W ; was born (past) - **2**. W ; it often rains (general truth) - **3**. W ; they're going - **4**. R ; *is always complaining* also possible - **5**. R - **6**. W ; I read (habit) - **7**. R - **8**. R - **9**. R - **10**. W ; he seems - **11**. R - **12**. W ; I like (verb expressing feeling)

2. **1**. 's probably watching / 's always lying - **2**. is cooking / cooks - **3**. are you going / is / ask / 're going - **4**. see / you're wearing / Are you going / 'm going / 's getting - **5**. is playing / don't like / sounds - **6**. Do you work / Do you come / do you take / are you leaving - **7**. wants / plan / are planning

9 PRESENT SIMPLE / CONTINUOUS (2)

1. Put the verbs in brackets in the present simple or continuous.

1. The children are very quiet. Go and see what they (do) ....

2. You (enjoy) .... the party or would you rather leave now? I (enjoy) .... myself very much, but it won't be long before I (leave) ...., because I (still suffer) .... from jet lag.

3. How you (get) .... to work, as a rule? I usually (go) .... by bus, but because of the strike, I (have) .... to take my car, which I (hate) .... I (hate) .... driving and getting stuck in traffic jams for hours on end.

4. How much you (owe) .... him? I (owe) .... him about fifty dollars. You (intend) .... to pay him back?

5. I always (buy) .... lottery tickets but I have never won anything.

6. You (dream) ....? Yes, I always (dream) .... and if I (eat) .... too much cheese, I (have) .... nightmares.

7. French workers are never satisfied. They always (complain) ....

8. How often you (write) .... to him? Well, I (write) .... every once in a while, but it's his birthday, so that's why I (write) .... a card.

9. Frankie and Johnnie (have) .... a long conversation. I (wonder) .... what on earth they (talk) .... about.

10. This moped (make) .... a strange noise. You (think) .... it's all right? Oh, that noise (not matter) .... It always (make) .... a noise like that, especially when I (forget) .... to top up the engine oil.

2. Write sentences using present continuous. Change the context when necessary as example in 1.

1. *She goes to the doctor's every other month.* ➭ *She's going to the doctor's this afternoon because she doesn't feel well.*

2. What do you do on Saturdays? I usually go shopping with mother.

....

3. The bargains this mall offers at Christmas are quite awesome.

....

4. We don't go abroad every summer.

....

5. She spends her spare time reading 19th century novels.

....

6. These premises are patrolled by guard dogs.

....

Correction

1. **1**. are doing - **2**. Are you enjoying / 'm enjoying / leave / 'm still suffering - **3**. do you get / usually go / have / hate / hate - **4**. do you owe / owe / Do you intend - **5**. I always buy - **6**. Do you dream / I always dream / eat / have - **7**. They are always complaining - **8**. do you write / write / 'm writing - **9**. are having / wonder / are talking - **10**. is making / Do you think / doesn't matter / makes / forget

2.

1. *She goes to the doctor's every other month.* ⇨ *She's going to the doctor's this afternoon because she doesn't feel well.*

2. What do you do on Saturdays? I usually go shopping with mother.
⇨ *But today I'm going to my friend's birthday party.*

3. The bargains this mall offers at Christmas are quite awesome.
⇨ *This Christmas, the shops are offering special rebates on all items.*

4. We don't go abroad every summer.
⇨ *This summer I'm going to the Alps.*

5. She spends her spare time reading 19th century novels.
⇨ *She's reading* Wuthering Heights *right now.*

6. These premises are patrolled by guard dogs.
⇨ *After last night's incidents, the riot police are patrolling the city round the clock.*

10 PRESENT PERFECT

1. Circle the letter of the correct answer. (English / French)

1. She's worked since the age of 21. ⇨ *Elle ... depuis l'âge de 21 ans.*
a) *travaille* b) *travaillait* c) *avait travaillé*

2. She's been driving for hours. ⇨ *Elle ... depuis des heures.*
a) *conduisait* b) *conduisit* c) *conduit*

3. The cat died three days ago. ⇨ *Le chat ... trois jours.*
a) *est mort depuis* b) *est mort il y a* c) *mourut en*

4. I've always loved sport. ⇨ *J' ... le sport.*
a) *aime toujours* b) *aimais bien* c) *ai toujours aimé*

5. I've lost my keys. ⇨ *... mes clés.*
a) *J'avais perdu* b) *Je perdis* c) *J'ai perdu*

2. Circle the letter of the correct answer. (French / English)

1. *As-tu déjeuné ?*
⇨ ... lunch?
a) Have you had b) Did you have c) Are you having

2. *(Où est Tom ?) Il est parti déjeuner.*
⇨ ... out for lunch.
a) He went b) He's gone c) He'd gone

3. *Elle sait conduire depuis qu'elle a 18 ans.*
⇨ She ... to drive since she was 18.
a) 's been able b) is able c) was able

4. *(Ça suffit.) Tu en as eu assez.* ⇨ You ... enough.
a) 've had b) had c) 've got

5. *Le garçonnet a disparu depuis longtemps.*
⇨ The little boy ... missing for a long time.
a) was b) had been c) 's been

6. *Il a arrêté de fumer depuis deux jours.* ⇨
a) He has been stopping smoking for two days.
b) He stopped smoking two days ago.
c) He has stopped smoking two days ago.

7. *Vous êtes déjà allé en Floride?* ⇨
a) Did you already go to Florida?
b) Have you ever been to Florida?
c) Had you been to Florida?

8. *C'est la troisième fois que l'école est détruite par un incendie.* ⇨
a) It has been the third time the school burns down.
b) It is the third time the school is burning down.
c) It's the third time the school has burnt down.

Correction

1. 1a - 2c - 3b - 4c - 5c

2. 1a - 2b - 3a - 4a - 5c - 6b - 7b - 8c

11 PRESENT PERFECT SIMPLE / CONTINUOUS

1. Combine the numbered elements with the lettered ones.

1. Look, the bottle is empty!	
2. It smells in here.	
3. The phone has been cut off.	
4. How nice to see you again!	
5. You're all wet.	
6. She isn't in.	
7. I've been trying to learn Arabic for years.	
8. She hasn't come in yet.	
9. He's phoned you three times this morning.	
10. He's been writing a novel for the past couple of weeks.	
11. He's away on business.	
12. I've lost my glasses again.	
13. There are no cigarettes left.	
14. John and Mary can't stand up straight.	

A. Have you seen them anywhere? **B**. You weren't home. **C**. She's gone to the movies. **D**. Someone has drunk all the wine. **E**. They've been trying to empty my wine cellar. **F**. I haven't paid my bill. **G**. I've been waiting for her for two hours. **H**. Judy's been smoking. **I**. Jane has smoked them all. **J**. Have you been playing out in the rain? **K**. Oh, is he? Where has he gone? **L**. I haven't succeeded yet. **M**. What have you been doing recently? **N**. He hasn't finished it yet.

2. Present perfect simple or continuous? Put the verbs in the correct form.

1. Since 1994 the world's economy (grow) .... by roughly 7% a year.

2. India (narrow) .... the gap between its growth and that of other Asian developing countries.

3. Airbags undoubtedly (save) .... thousands of lives. But they also (kill) .... a few people who would not otherwise have died.

4. Opinion polls suggest the opposition will defeat the ruling party, which (be) .... in power for 7 years.

5. Throughout their 5,000 years of recorded history, Egyptian farmers never (pay) .... for water.

6. In the past few decades, growing numbers of married women (take) .... paid jobs.

7. I (run) .... ten miles this morning. I'm exhausted.

Correction

1. 1D - 2H - 3F - 4M - 5J - 6C - 7L - 8G - 9B - 10N - 11K - 12A - 13I - 14E

2. **1**. has been growing - **2**. has narrowed - **3**. have undoubtedly saved / have also killed - **4**. has been - **5**. have never paid - **6**. have been taking - **7**. 've run

12 HAVE YOU BEEN / HAVE YOU DONE?

1. Spot the possible mistakes and correct them. Write R for Right.

1. R / W............... Hello Tim, I didn't see you for ages.
2. R / W............... The mechanic was working on the car for an hour now.
3. R / W............... I'm looking for my wallet. Did you see it?
4. R / W............... Did you ever climb on top of the Empire State Building?
5. R / W............... He was afraid of driving ever since his accident.
6. R / W............... Are you ever been to California?

2. Tick the right box (1= Present Perfect, 2 = Past). Translate.

	1	2	Traduction
1. *Quand as-tu acheté ce DVD ?*			
2. *Depuis combien de temps est-il hospitalisé ?*			
3. *Pendant combien de temps ont-ils négocié ?*			
4. *Depuis quand étudies-tu le piano ?*			
5. *Quand a-t-il commencé à pleuvoir ?*			
6. *Où as-tu garé le 4x4 hier soir ?*			
7. *As-tu vu le dernier film de Oliver Stone ?*			
8. *A-t-il déjeuné ?*			
9. *Tu as lu* The Snow Leopard *?*			
10. *Qui composa* La Flûte enchantée *?*			

3. Translate into good English.

1. *Tu as déjà rencontré sa nièce ?* ....
2. *Tu sais où il est parti ?* ....
3. *Es-tu déjà allé au Canada ?* ....
4. *Tu as lu la presse aujourd'hui ?* ....
5. *Vous avez fait de bonnes affaires cette année ?*
....
6. *Tu as pris ton café ?* ....
7. *Tu as pris des vacances récemment?* ....
8. *Qu'est-ce qui s'est passé ?* ....
9. *Qui a mangé les fraises ?* ....
10. *Tu t'es déjà fait prendre par un radar ?* ....

Correction

1. **1**. I haven't seen you - **2**. has been working - **3**. Have you seen it - **4**. Have you ever climbed - **5**. He's been afraid of... - **6**. Have you ever been

2.

	1	2
1. *Quand as-tu acheté ce DVD ?*		x
2. *Depuis combien de temps est-il hospitalisé ?*	x	
3. *Pendant combien de temps ont-ils négocié ?*		x
4. *Depuis quand étudies-tu le piano ?*	x	
5. *Quand a-t-il commencé à pleuvoir ?*		x
6. *Où as-tu garé le 4x4 hier soir ?*		x
7. *As-tu vu le dernier film de Oliver Stone ?*	x	
8. *A-t-il déjeuné ?*	x	
9. *Tu as lu* The Snow Leopard *?*	x	
10. *Qui composa* La Flûte enchantée *?*		x

Translation

1. When did you buy this DVD?
2. How long has he been in hospital for?
3. How long did they negotiate for?
4. How long have you been studying the piano?
5. When did it start raining?
6. Where did you park the SUV last night?
7. Have you seen Oliver Stone's latest film?
8. Has he had lunch?
9. Have you read *The Snow Leopard*?
10. Who wrote *The Magic Flute*?

3. **1**. Have you ever met his sister? **2**. Do you know where he's gone? **3**. Have you ever been to Canada? **4**. Have you read the papers today? **5**. Have you had a good year business-wise? **6**. Have you had your coffee? **7**. Have you taken a holiday recently? **8**. What's happened? **9**. Who's eaten the strawberries? **10**. Have you ever been caught in a radar speed-trap?

13 PAST SIMPLE

1. Spot the possible mistakes and correct them. Write R for Right.

1. R / W............... It's the first time he visited the US. He'd never been there before.
2. R / W............... Did you have lunch yet?
3. R / W............... Greg is born in Denver.
4. R / W............... He traveled a lot when he was young.
5. R / W............... He lived in Dresden since the end of the war.
6. R / W............... He lived in Durham for several years.
7. R / W............... When have you gone to Vienna?
8. R / W............... I have met him last week.
9. R / W............... Nixon has resigned in 1974.
10. R / W............... The train has already left. You've missed it.
11. R / W............... Whole cities have been destroyed during WW2.
12. R / W............... Why haven't you come last Sunday?

2. Complete the sentences using verbs from the list.

become / begin / catch / cut / fall / freeze / have / know / lose / see

1. It started to rain and he .... to take shelter under some pine trees. **2**. What (you) .... your finger with? **3**. I .... he was my long-lost brother the minute I .... him. **4**. What with the temperature dropping below zero, no wonder he .... a cold playing outside with just a sweater on! **5**. Last winter was particularly harsh and many homeless .... to death. **6**. The little boy .... over while crossing the street. **7**. Many people .... all their money in the 1929 Wall Street crash. **8**. Mozart .... to compose when he was five and .... a boy-wonder, a virtuoso on both the harpsichord and violin.

3. Complete the sentences using *since / for / ago*.

1. She played competition tennis ...... ten years and then retired from the game in 2007. **2**. It's two years ...... we last visited Italy. **3**. After our quarrel, she didn't speak to me ...... three weeks. **4**. How long ...... did you arrive in Provincetown? **5**. I haven't seen her ...... we met a year ago. **6**. After his accident, he was kept in hospital ...... two months. He has ...... made a complete recovery. **7**. She was born seventeen years .... **8**. He studied the piano ...... fifteen years before giving his first concert. **9**. It is thirty years ...... the exiled king last set foot in his home country. **10**. Smallpox was eradicated several years ....

Correction

1. **1**. It was - **2**. Have you had - **3**. was born (past) - **4**. R - **5**. He has been living (since = beginning of action) - **6**. R (lack of context : past tense) - **7**. did you go (when = pronoun, ex. two years ago / last month / in 1997, etc.) - **8**. met (date) - **9**. resigned (date) - **10**. R - **11**. were destroyed (the war's over) - **12**. didn't you come (date)

2. **1**. had - **2**. did you cut - **3**. knew / saw - **4**. caught - **5**. froze - **6**. fell - **7**. lost - **8**. began / became

3. **1**. for - **2**. since - **3**. for - **4**. ago - **5**. since - **6**. for / since - **7**. ago - **8**. for - **9**. since - **10**. ago

14 PAST SIMPLE / CONTINUOUS

1. Spot the possible mistakes and correct them. Write R for Right.

1. R / W............... He was always smirking when he was hearing her.
2. R / W............... I was knowing him quite well when we were at school.
3. R / W............... Jane was loving Gary for a long time before they eventually got married.
4. R / W............... He was making a speech. Hecklers kept interrupting him.
5. R / W............... The boat was sailing in the Red Sea for two weeks when it was hijacked by pirates.
6. R / W............... I was thinking of inviting them to my farewell party.
7. R / W............... Robin was catching the 6 o'clock flight, so she thought she'd better rush.
8. R / W............... Somebody stole my wallet while I was seeing the sights.

2. Put the verbs in the correct tense.

1. According to the warden, the prisoner (escape) .... through the sewer. **2**. He (watch) .... *ET* when there was a knock on the door. **3**. She (grill) .... sardines. Suddenly her dress (catch) .... fire. **4**. The last time I (see) .... him, he (renovate) .... an old barn. **5**. As she (exit) .... the lot, a cab (ram) .... into her SUV. **6**. She said she (have) .... a sandwich at the office and could not see me. **7**. He (walk) .... across the street when he (knock) .... down by a bus. **8**. The *Titanic* (sail) .... across the Atlantic when she (hit) .... an iceberg and (sink) .... in barely three hours.

3. Circle the letter of the correct answer.

1. When she arrived <u>we were having lunch</u>.
a) nous étions en train de déjeuner - b) nous déjeunâmes
2. When she arrived <u>we had lunch</u>.
a) nous déjeunâmes - b) nous déjeunions
3. He <u>was being operated on</u> when the lights went out.
a) on l'opéra - b) on l'opérait
4. <u>I was constantly being disturbed</u> by the ringing of the phone.
a) On est en train de me déranger - b) J'étais constamment dérangé
5. The mechanic <u>was trying</u> to fix the engine.
a) essaya - b) essayait

Correction

1. **1**. heard - **2**. knew - **3**. had been in love / had loved her - **4**. R - **5**. had been sailing / had sailed - **6**. R - **7**. R - **8**. R ; was seeing the sights = *faire du tourisme*

2. **1**. escaped - **2**. was watching - **3**. was grilling / caught - **4**. saw / was renovating - **5**. was exiting / rammed - **6**. was having - **7**. was walking / was knocked - **8**. was sailing / hit / sank

3. 1a - 2a - 3b - 4b - 5b

15 PRESENT PERFECT / PAST (1)

Circle the letter of the correct answer.

1. "Have you ever visited the Bahamas?" — "Yes, I ... there last year."
a) was going b) have been
c) have been going d) went

2. Inflation ... since last Spring, but then it gradually started leveling off.
a) rose b) has risen c) was rising d) had been rising

3. Never before ... the men's 100-meter dash run like this.
a) saw the world b) the world saw
c) the world has seen d) has the world seen

4. Isn't it time he ... crying like a baby?
a) has stopped b) stopped c) stops d) is stopping

5. How long ago ... his first album?
a) has he cut b) did he cut c) he had cut d) he cut

6. He was as excited as if ... the first time he'd taken a girl out.
a) it had been b) it could be
c) it should be d) it has been

7. As you can see, a great deal of money ... into the refurbishing of the new museum.
a) went b) is going c) was gone d) has gone

8. Do you know what happened to them the last time they ... in Iran?
a) went b) were c) have been d) have gone

9. It will be the first time a woman ... for the highest office in the land.
a) was running b) had been running
c) has run d) is running

10. I ... three movies this past fortnight.
a) have been seeing b) am seeing
c) have seen d) see

11. In such circumstances, I'd rather ... the idea.
a) giving up b) give up c) to give up d) should give up

12. Boy! You ... since the last time I last saw you.
a) grew b) were growing
c) had grown d) have grown

13. We ... each other for 15 years. We still get together once in a while.
a) 'd known b) 've known
c) knew d) 've been knowing

14. Look! I don't care if you ... the bus this morning. You're fired!
a) miss b) 've missed c) were missing d) 'd missed

15. I ... the same car for more than ten years. It still works fine.
a) 've had b) 've got c) 'd got d) got

Correction

1d ; date (last year = past tense) - **2b** - **3d** ; inversion after negative adverb ; present perfect with *never* - **4b** ; past modal (*it's time / high time / about time*) - **5b** ; past tense with *ago* - **6a** ; past modal (*as if*) - **7d** ; *as you can see* requires present perfect - **8b** ; past tense with *last time* - **9c** ; *the first / second / third time* + present perfect - **10c** ; action which started in the past and is not completed (*this past fortnight*) - **11b** ; past modal with *I'd rather (+ he / she / you / they)* - **12d** - **13b** - **14b** - **15a**

16 PRESENT PERFECT / PAST (2)

1. Combine the numbered sentences with the lettered ones.

1. They played music for three hours last night with the windows wide open. ......
2. She left her mobile phone on the commuter train. ......
3. I haven't seen that film yet. ......
4. The children haven't come downstairs yet. ......
5. The flight from Rio hasn't come in yet. ......
6. I've tried to explain the situation to Jane. ......
7. I planted those rose-trees last winter. ......
8. Do you know anyone who's ever won on a lottery? ......
9. Look! The Joneses have bought a new BMW. ......
10. I've made a reservation for you too. ......

A. But I plan to go next week. **B**. No, that's why I've never bought a ticket. **C**. No wonder the neighbours have been complaining. **D**. She won't listen. **E**. It's nice to see them in full bloom. **F**. They must still be in bed. **G**. Thank heavens for that! **H**. It might have been delayed by the blizzard. **I**. I hope you'll be able to come. **J**. They must be rolling in it!

2. Put the verbs in brackets in the correct tense.

1. I (not see) .... you since last Monday. Where have you been?
2. I (take) .... my Sunday stroll when I happened to bump into an old flame.
3. I used to love playing tennis, but (give up) .... it now.
4. The car (sit) .... out in the drive since it broke down.
5. She's been trying to get me to go out for dinner for three weeks but I (be) .... too busy.
6. I (break) .... my glasses while playing rugby. I guess I'll have to buy a new pair.
7. My children (have) .... all mumps.
8. The company (go) .... bankrupt shortly after its manager died in 2005.
9. The president managed to come back from the dead when he (hire) .... a new spin doctor.
10. Ever since his political comeback, he (ride) .... high in the popularity ratings.
11. Since they (know) .... each other, they have got on like a house on fire.

Correction

1. 1C - 2G - 3A - 4F - 5H - 6D - 7E - 8B - 9J - 10I

2. **1**. haven't seen - **2**. was taking - **3**. have given it up - **4**. has been sitting - **5**. 've been - **6**. broke - **7**. have all had - **8**. went - **9**. hired - **10**. 's been riding - **11**. have known

17 PRESENT PERFECT / PAST (3)

1. Write sentences using words in brackets.

1. (I / not play chess / with my neighbor / since / I / come back / from Russia / last month)

....

2. (Prince Harry / state / during a press conference / he / sue *The Sun*)

....

3. (Where / you / be?) (I / be / to the sales / Look at / these lovely socks / I / buy / you!)

....

4. (Where on earth / you / put / the paper? / I / not read it yet)

....

5. (Since / he / become mayor / local taxes / rise / twice already)

....

6. (The band / give / a farewell concert / the day before yesterday)

....

7. (The bomb / go off / at dawn / according to the authorities / many people / be killed in the blast)

....

2. Put the adverbs in brackets in the correct position (a / b / c). Circle the right letter.

1. Over the years, civil liberties **(a)** have been **(b)** eroded **(c)** by a stream of new laws. (**GRADUALLY**)
2. International scrutiny of Britain's human rights record **(a)** has **(b)** become **(c)** critical. (**INCREASINGLY**)
3. Complete freedom of capital movement has **(a)** been **(b)** achieved **(c)** throughout the European Union. (**RECENTLY**)
4. Today, the ratio of active workers to retired people **(a)** has fallen **(b)** — and is **(c)** narrowing. (**SHARPLY / RAPIDLY**)
5. Sexually, the British **(a)** have become **(b)** permissive **(c)** in recent years, despite the emergence of AIDS in the 1980s. (**INCREASINGLY**)
6. We have **(a)** known **(b)** how evil and murderous the Nazis were **(c)**. (**ALWAYS**)
7. The past years' reforms **(a)** have **(b)** improved **(c)** India's economic prospects. (**VASTLY**)
8. The country **(a)** has **(b)** changed — in its big cities, **(c)** so. (**VISIBLY / STRIKINGLY**)

Correction

1. **1**. I've not played chess with my neighbor since I came back from Russia last month. **2**. Prince Harry stated during a press conference that he would sue *The Sun*. **3**. "Where have you been?" "I've been to the sales. Look at these lovely socks I've bought you!" **4**. Where on earth have you put the paper? I haven't read it yet. **5**. Since he became mayor, local taxes have risen twice already. **6**. The band gave a farewell concert the day before yesterday. **7**. The bomb went off at dawn. According to the authorities many people were killed in the blast.

2. **1c**. Over the years, civil liberties have been **gradually** eroded by a stream of new laws. **2c**. International scrutiny of Britain's human rights record has become **increasingly** critical. **3a**. Complete freedom of capital movement has **recently** been achieved throughout the European Union. **4b/c**. Today, the ratio of active workers to retired people has fallen **sharply** — and is **rapidly** narrowing. **5b**. Sexually, the British have become **increasingly** liberal in recent years, despite the emergence of AIDS in the 1980s. **6a**. We have **always** known how evil and murderous the Nazis were. **7b**. The past years' reforms have **vastly** improved India's economic prospects. **8b/c**. The country has **visibly** changed — in its big cities, **strikingly** so.

18 PAST / PRESENT PERFECT (1)

1. **Write T (True) or F (False) for the statement that follows each numbered sentence.**

1. When they left Vienna, it started to rain.
It was raining when they were in Vienna : ....

2. When he finally got to school, his class was taking a test.
He arrived to school on time for the test : ......

3. While he was buying his magazine, he met an old friend.
He finished buying his magazine. Then he met his friend : ......

4. As I was doing the shopping, somebody picked my wallet.
When he got to the cash desk he was unable to pay for his errands : ......

5. When it stopped snowing she drove to her parents'.
She drove to her parents after it had stopped snowing : ......

6. Have you ever seen the movie?
I want to know how often you go to the cinema : ......

7. She's visited New York several times.
She knows the city like the back of her hand : ......

2. **Combine the numbered elements with the lettered ones.**

1. As the faucet has been leaking for two weeks now, ...
2. As you haven't had lunch yet, ...
3. They have developed a good vaccine against the flu, so ......
4. When I last saw you ......
5. I've cleared the drive of snow, so ......
6. The grass is all scorched. ......
7. I'm out of breath. ......
8. Do you think that will be enough? ......
9. He's been to Spain for his vacation. ......

a. It hasn't rained for weeks.
b. Look! He's so tanned.
c. they have called the plumber.
d. I've exercised for two hours.
e. I think you ought to have your jab.
f. My feet are freezing.
g. you must be starving.
h. I've made several sandwiches.
i. you said you would never marry a Scot.

Correction

1. 1F - 2F - 3F - 4T - 5T - 6F - 7T

2. 1c - 2g - 3e - 4i - 5f - 6a - 7d - 8h - 9b

19 PAST / PRESENT PERFECT (2)

Write T (True) or F (False) for the statement that follows each numbered sentence.

1. They owned the local factory from 2003 to 2008.
They sold their business : ......

2. They've decided to live apart.
The decision has been made recently : ......

3. They have lived apart for three years.
They are still living apart : ......

4. I've had several cups of coffee this morning.
It's still morning : ......

5. He's been collecting old postcards since the age of five.
He no longer collects them : ......

6. She's been working on her dissertation for two years.
Her dissertation is finished : ......

7. It's been raining for several days.
It's still raining : ......

8. His novel has been selling like hot cakes.
It is no longer on the best-selling list : ......

9. I've read an interesting book about comets.
I've finished reading the book : ......

10. She's been writing an article for *Science Magazine*.
She's still writing the article : ......

11. The drought victims have been waiting for relief supplies for two weeks.
They have finally got their supplies : ......

12. They have been living in San Francisco since the turn of the century.
They are still living there : ......

13. He has given several talks about wildlife preservation.
He's an expert in his field : ......

14. He's been studying at Harvard.
He's no longer a student : ......

15. The manager's out for lunch.
The store is closed for the day : ......

Correction

1T - 2T - 3T - 4T - 5F - 6F - 7T - 8F - 9T - 10T - 11F - 12T - 13T - 14F - 15F

20 PAST PERFECT

1. Put the verbs in brackets in the correct tense.

1. I (never see) .... such pristine beaches before I visited the Maldives.
2. The Smiths were unable to find a hotel room because they (not book) .... in advance.
3. She was able to show the visitors around LA because she (spend) .... three years there as a student.
4. Angelina (never go) .... to a play before last night.
5. He was reluctant to sell the house because his parents (live) .... there for twenty years.
6. He (try) .... to hitch a lift for two hours when at last somebody stopped to pick him up.
7. He wished he (emigrate) .... to the USA when he was younger.
8. He had been stuck in a jam and by the time he arrived to his office the meeting already (start) ....
9. I would have reimbursed you once I (pay) ....

2. Put the verbs in brackets in the correct tense.

The Fatal Shore

In 1787, in the twenty-eighth year of the reign of King George III, the British government (send) .... out a fleet to colonise Australia.
Never (found) .... a colony so far from its parent state, or in such ignorance of the land it (occupy) .... There (be) .... no reconnaissance. In 1770, Captain James Cook (make) .... landfall on the unexplored east coast of this utterly enigmatic continent, (stop) .... for a short while at a place named Botany Bay and (sail) .... northwards. Since then, no ship (call) ....: not a word, not an observation, for seventeen years, each one of which (be) .... exactly like the thousands that (precede) .... it, locked in its historical immensity of blue heat, sandstone and the measured booming of glassy Pacific rollers.
Now this coast (be to) .... witness a new colonial experiment, never tried before, not repeated since. An unexplored continent would become a jail. The space around it, the very air and sea, the whole transparent labyrinth of the South Pacific, would become a wall 14,000 miles thick.

Robert Hughes, *The Fatal Shore: The Epic of Australia's Founding*, Vintage Books, Random House, New York, 1986 (adapted).

Correction

1. **1**. had never seen - **2**. had not booked - **3**. had spent - **4**. had never gone - **5**. had lived - **6**. had been trying - **7**. had emigrated - **8**. had already started - **9**. had been paid

2. In 1787, in the twenty-eighth year of the reign of King George III, the British government **sent** out a fleet to colonise Australia.

Never **had** a colony **been founded** so far from its parent state, or in such ignorance of the land it **occupied**. There **had been** no reconnaissance. In 1770, Captain James Cook **had made** landfall on the unexplored east coast of this utterly enigmatic continent, **stopped** for a short while at a place named Botany Bay and **sailed** northwards. Since then, no ship **had called** : not a word, not an observation, for seventeen years, each one of which **was** exactly like the thousands that **had preceded** it, locked in its historical immensity of blue heat, sandstone and the measured booming of glassy Pacific rollers.

Now this coast **was to** witness a new colonial experiment, never tried before, not repeated since. An unexplored continent would become a jail. The space around it, the very air and sea, the whole transparent labyrinth of the South Pacific, would become a wall 14,000 miles thick.

21 PAST / PAST PERFECT (1)

Circle the letter of the correct answer.

1. It was the most far-reaching project ... .
a) they haven't undertaken yet b) they have still undertaken
c) they were always undertaking d) they had ever undertaken

2. Greg ... in Berlin for 20 years then he decided to move to Rome.
a) lived b) lives c) has lived d) has been living

3. "Sun flowers" ... painted towards the end of Van Gogh's life.
a) was b) has been c) ø d) would be

4. The President declared: "It's time we ... the federal budget".
a) reduce b) reduced c) would reduce d) will reduce

5. It ... the third time he ... a firm since ... from California.
a) was / sold / arrived b) was / had sold / arriving
c) is / sold / arriving d) is / had sold / arriving

6. Their decision immediately created an urgent problem which nobody in the firm ... .
a) thought b) would have thought about
c) was thinking d) had thought about

7. When the rescue team finally arrived on the spot he ... for an hour.
a) had died b) was dying c) had been dead d) has been dead

8. It's high time we ... if we want to catch the red-eye flight.
a) leave b) left c) are leaving d) have left

9. When we went to Niagara Falls last year, it was the first time I ... such breath-taking scenery.
a) would see b) had seen c) was seeing d) have seen

10. "What ... for dinner last night?", asked the doctor.
a) have you eaten b) did you eat
c) have you been eating d) were you eating

11. She heaped scorn on him as if he ... the lowest of the low.
a) be b) is c) were d) had been

12. She watched a video after she ... the children to bed.
a) puts b) was putting c) had put d) has put

13. If only he ... to my advice, he would not be in such a predicament today.
a) listened b) had listened c) was listening d) has listened

14. ... he would have been able to catch his plane.
a) Did he hurry b) Should he hurry
c) If he hurries d) Had he hurried

15. They rang to say they would be late - they ... the bus.
a) missed b) have missed c) had missed d) would miss

Correction

1d - **2a** ; for = *pendant* (past) - **3a** ; date (= past tense) - **4b** ; past modal (*it's time / I'd rather you / I wish / if only*) - **5b** ; it is the first time + present perfect ÷ it was the third time + past perfect - **6d** - **7c** ; do not confuse to die ÷ to be dead - **8b** ; cf question 4 - **9b** - **10b** ; date - **11c** ; cf question 4 - **12c** - **13b** - **14b** - **15c**

22 PAST / PAST PERFECT (2)

1. Spot the possible mistakes and correct them. Write R for Right.

1. R / W............... He said he would buy a new car as soon as he has found the money.
2. R / W............... We would buy the house if the price had been right.
3. R / W............... Hardly started the quiz when there was a bomb scare.
4. R / W............... When she got back home she realized that her flat had been broken into.
5. R / W............... It is ten years since he had last been back home.
6. R / W............... He looked out of the window: it was raining; it was raining for half an hour.
7. R / W............... The high-speed train was traveling at full speed when it hit a concrete block which laid on the tracks.
8. R / W............... They had had to close down the factory because it was no longer considered profitable.
9. R / W............... The country was hit by a drought two years before. It was the third time within a decade that the crops had been to suffer.
10. R / W............... Since the demise of communism, tourists had been swarming over the city every summer, bringing with them hard cash but also pollution and vandalism.

2. Put the verbs in brackets in the past or present perfect tense.

1. When they had successfully concluded talks, the union leaders and managers (shake) .... hands and (go) .... their separate ways.
2. They (not / finish) .... building the sports arena when it was inaugurated.
3. When he was young, he (like) .... collecting butterflies and stamps.
4. After she had been operated on, she (take) .... a few days' rest and then (go) .... back to work.
5. He told the journalist that he (smoke) .... marijuana when a student, but he (not / inhale) ....
6. He used to spend his holidays in the same quaint little village in Brittany as I did but we never (meet) ....
7. Although he had traveled extensively in his youth, he never (set) .... foot in the Outer Hebrides.
8. He had been looking for a job since he (graduate) .... from high school but always (tell) .... that he lacked experience.
9. He (save) .... up for a rainy day but his wife's illness swallowed up what little money he had put aside.
10. He (not / see) .... her since she moved to New England.

Correction

1. **1**. as soon as he found : time clause - **2**. we would have bought ; if-clause - **3**. Hardly had the quiz started ; inversion following semi-negative adverbs (*hardly / no sooner / seldom*, etc.) - **4**. R - **5**. It was ; note : it is + present perfect ÷ it was + past perfect - **6**. it had been raining ; action in the past ; for = *depuis* (past perfect here) - **7**. had been laid ; note the difference between to lie (no object), and to lay, (+ object) ; to lie / lay / lain ÷ to lay / laid / laid - **8**. R - **9**. had been hit ; were to suffer - **10**. have been swarming also possible

2. **1**. shook / went - **2**. hadn't finished - **3**. liked - **4**. took / went - **5**. had smoked / had not inhaled - **6**. never met - **7**. had never set - **8**. graduated / had always been told - **9**. had been saving - **10**. had not seen

23 PAST PERFECT SIMPLE / CONTINUOUS

1. Write sentences using elements in brackets.

1. The little girl had been missing since November.
➩ (The police / look for her / for several months).
....

2. The French students were discontented.
➩ (There / be / unrest / since the beginning of the fall semester).
....

3. There were warnings of a hurricane in Florida.
➩ (People / shore up / houses / since the first warnings / go out).
....

4. South L.A. looked like a wasteland after the flare-up of violence.
➩ (The Blacks and the Hispanics / riot / for several days).
....

5. The space station had been damaged in a collision with a supply ship.
➩ (For two days / the crew / work round the clock / to repair the damage).
....

2. Indicate the form of the verb (past simple / continuous).

1. He said that in his youth he often (live) .... abroad. He (live) .... in Spain, Greece and the United States. **2**. When the police finally arrived on the scene he (be dead) .... for an hour. **3**. Until his resignation last month, he (be) .... defence minister for two years. **4**. They (negotiate) .... for weeks before they finally reached an agreement. **5**. She signaled that she wanted to have a seat because she (stand) .... on her feet all day long. **6**. He (work) .... for the same company for 25 years when it went out of business. **7**. No wonder he was tired! He (exercise) .... so hard to lose weight. **8**. The house (belong) .... to a famous poet before it was sold.

3. Put the verb in the correct tense (past / past perfect simple, continuous).

1. The farmer (feel) .... suicidal. He was going to have to sell the farm where his family (toil) .... all their lives. **2**. We (walk) .... to the station when one of my wife's heels (break) .... and we had to go back home and change her shoes. **3**. She asked him to repeat the question. At her age, she said, she (not / hear) .... very well. **4**. Scenes from his all-too-short life (flash) .... through his mind as he (drown) .... **5**. While I out (shop) .... , someone broke into my home.

Correction

1. **1**. The police had been looking for her for several months. **2**. There had been unrest since the beginning of the fall semester. **3**. People had been shoring up their houses since the first warnings had gone out. **4**. The Blacks and the Hispanics had been rioting for several days. **5**. For two days the crew had been working round the clock to repair the damage.

2. **1**. had often lived / had lived - **2**. had been dead - **3**. had been - **4**. had been negotiating - **5**. had been standing - **6**. had been working - **7**. had been exercising - **8**. had belonged

3. **1**. was feeling / had toiled - **2**. were walking / broke - **3**. could not hear - **4**. flashed / was drowning - **5**. was out shopping

24 PAST MODAL / PAST PERFECT MODAL

1. Write sentences using *it's time / it's high time.*

1. He's been working like a dog for two years now. ➪ (take a vacation)

....

2. They haven't repainted my office since 1979. The electricity and the plumbing are faulty. ➪ (renovate / give a lick of paint / redo the plumbing / rewire the place)

....

3. Your hair is too long and you haven't shaved for weeks. ➪ (have it cut / buy a razor)

....

4. They have been on strike for two months. ➪ (resume work)

....

2. Complete sentences using *'d rather* + past / past perfect modal.

1. Don't tell them about our project. (I / they / not know)

....

2. Why have you come so late? (I / you / come earlier)

....

3. Why did you repair my bike? (I / you / buy me a new one)

....

4. I must get up very early tomorrow. (I / rather / not go to bed)

....

5. The police has his passport. (They / rather / he not leave the country for now)

....

3. Put the verbs in brackets in the correct tense.

1. You look as if you (can / do) .... with a drink right now. **2**. Suppose the beach guard (not dive in) ....? The little boy would surely have drowned. **3**. If he had not swum so far, he (not get caught) .... in the fast current. **4**. If the fire (spread) .... to the refinery it would have been a disaster. **5**. I would have been grateful if you (can / send) .... me a copy of your latest catalogue. **6**. We bought some food in case the children (come) .... **7**. He left his widow a fortune on condition she (not / remarry) .... **8**. Suppose George W. Bush (not / elect) .... in 2000, Al Gore would have become president. **9**. "A glass of white wine?" "No, thanks, I'd rather (have) .... an orange juice." **10**. I wish I (bring) .... my binoculars. I could have followed the regatta from the balcony of my hotel room.

Correction

1. **1**. It's time he took a vacation. **2**. It's time they renovated it / it were renovated / they gave it a lick of paint / they redid the plumbing / they rewired the place / the place were rewired. **3**. It's time you had it cut / you bought a razor. **4**. It's time they resumed work.

2. **1**. I'd rather they didn't know. **2**. I'd rather you had come earlier. **3**. I'd rather you had bought me a new one. **4**. I'd rather not go to bed. **5**. They'd rather he didn't leave the country for now.

3. **1**. could do - **2**. had not dived in - **3**. would not have got caught - **4**. had spread - **5**. could have sent - **6**. came - **7**. didn't remarry - **8**. hadn't been elected - **9**. have - **10**. had brought

25 USED TO

1. Put *use* in the right format.

1. Try to clean this pan without .... scouring powder.
2. He has promised not .... the bath towels to clean his shoes with any more.
3. Anyone can get .... anything, if he tries hard enough.
4. I .... like this music at all, but I've changed since I began going to concerts.
5. The country .... be plagued by daily "brown outs" which often lasted for eight hours or more.
6. The country's problems of drinking water are at least as bad as they .... be in electricity.
7. There are 25 East Caribbean volcanoes, most looking just as harmless as they ...., which could one day explode.
8. The children had become fractious and grumpy because they .... staying up late.

2. Make sentences with words in brackets using *used to*.

1. Today, I always travel light. ➪ (carry / lots of luggage)
....
2. I love broccoli and zucchinis. ➪ (hate / vegetables)
....
3. He no longer goes skiing. He's past it now. ➪ (when he was young / go skiing / at least twice a year)
....
4. I only subscribe to a couple of magazines. ➪ (take / at least ten of them)
....
5. Since we moved out to the country we no longer go to the cinema much. ➪ (go / twice a week / when I lived in London)
....

3. Ask questions.

1. Every summer we used to drive down to Cape Cod. ....
2. He used to sing in a choir before his voice broke. ....
3. There used to be a grandfather clock in Granny's house. ....
4. Telephones used to have dials. ....

Correction

1. **1**. using - **2**. to use - **3**. get used to - **4**. didn't use(d) to - **5**. used to - **6**. used to - **7**. used to - **8**. were not used to staying

2. **1**. I used to carry lots of luggage. **2**. I used to hate vegetables. **3**. He used to go skiing at least twice a year when he was young. **4**. I used to take at least ten of them. **5**. We used to go twice a week when I lived in London.

3. **1**. Did you use to drive down to Cape Cod? **2**. Did he use to sing in a choir before his voice broke? **3**. Did there use to be a grandfather clock in Granny's house? **4**. Did telephones use to have dials?

26 USED TO / BE USED TO

1. Spot the possible mistakes and correct them. Write R for Right.

1. R / W.............. Can you give me a hand? I'm not used to use this particular video-recorder.
2. R / W.............. Andrew, who used to living in Aberdeen, was recently transferred to Singapore by his firm.
3. R / W.............. He had used to read a lot of comic strips when he was younger but fortunately he has now grown out of such a childish habit.
4. R / W.............. It used to being said in Washington that anyone who is anyone is probably a lawyer.
5. R / W.............. When our daughter was in her teens, we were used to have endless rows. Now, however, we get on like a house on fire.
6. R / W.............. I used to do a lot of gardening until I started getting chronic backache.
7. R / W.............. When we were out in the West, we used to driving down long, empty interstates. Now that we're back in Europe, we're finding it hard getting used to the overcrowded roads.

2. Complete the sentences with *used to*, *get used to* or *be used to* (+ verb).

1. In my early years in the industry, I (not consider) .... as a promising actor. **2**. At the turn of last century, very few women (go) .... out to work. WWI changed all that. **3**. In those days he (play) .... the trumpet for hours a day. **4**. Like most politicians, he has the gift of the gab. He (make) .... speeches. **5**. After two years in New York, Jean-Pierre now (eat) .... American food. **6**. Refugees often (use) .... as weapons of war by unscrupulous leaders.

3. Complete the sentences with *use* in the right format.

1. At the present moment the same routes .... to get drugs across the border. **2**. A major breakthrough in the fight against breast cancer has just been made by scientists .... the venom of the copperhead snake. **3**. Americans value their free time more than they ...., and now demand greater reward for working overtime. **4**. A decade ago, millions of Americans were already .... computers, but few saw much .... for the Internet. **5**. No matter how hard they tried, the children never .... calling their stepfather Daddy. **6**. Farmers .... getting handouts, be they subsidies in the rich world or technology packages in poor countries. **7**. Where listening to music .... imply paying for concert tickets or owning a piano, the invention of the radio made music more accessible to everyone and virtually free.

Correction

1. **1**. I'm not used to using - **2**. used to live - **3**. used to read - **4**. used to be said - **5**. were used to having / used to have - **6**. R - **7**. got used to driving

2. **1**. wasn't used to being considered - **2**. used to go out - **3**. used to play - **4**. is used to making - **5**. has got used to eating - **6**. have often been used

3. **1**. are being used - **2**. using - **3**. used to - **4**. using / use - **5**. got used to - **6**. are used to - **7**. used to

27 USED TO / WOULD

1. Complete the sentences using *(be) used to* or *would*.

1. I .... be fond of detective novels. Now I just read the paper.
2. I .... snuggle up in bed at night and read late into the night.
3. While I was revising for my exams, I .... take half a day off to go and play tennis.
4. When I lived in Spain we .... to have dinner at 10 p.m.
5. I (not) .... to sleeping a lot.
6. Every once in a while, Pussy .... disappear and then turn up again, looking pleased with itself. We .... then place an ad in the local paper to find it.

2. Circle the letter of the correct answer.

1. I am not used ... such strong cigars!
a) to smoke b) smoking
c) having smoked d) to smoking

2. In those days he ... play golf for hours in a day.
a) was used to b) has used c) used to d) should

3. The embedded reporters complained to the authorities that they ... treated so shabbily.
a) were not used to being b) have used to be
c) used not be d) did not use to being

4. She ... sometimes call on us on her way home.
a) was using to b) was used to
c) would d) used

5. In my early years with the firm, I ... being considered as a VIP.
a) wasn't used to b) wasn't used
c) didn't use d) didn't use to

6. The Chinese government ... people out on the streets demonstrating for human rights.
a) is not used to seeing b) is not used to see
c) used not to see d) doesn't use to see

7. Steven ... a bottle of Burgundy a day. But those days are gone.
a) used to drinking b) were used to drink
c) would usually drink d) used to drinking

8. Britain ... have a strong manufacturing base. However, it now accounts for a mere twenty per cent of GNP.
a) was used to have b) was used to having
c) used to d) would

Correction

1. **1**. used to be ; contrast past / present - **2**. would ; past habit - **3**. would - **4**. used to - **5**. 'm not used to sleeping ; present habit - **6**. would / would ; repetition of an action in the past

2. **1d** ; present habit - **2c** ; past action (in those days = *à cette époque*) - **3a** - **4c** ; past habit (sometimes) - **5a** - **6a** - **7c** - **8c**

28 SINCE / FOR / AGO

1. Complete the sentences using *since* / *for* or *ago*.

1. ... medieval times, the coal beneath Northumberland has earned people a hard but steady living.

2. Ever ... it came to power 5 years ..., the left-wing coalition has been dabbling with tax reform, but almost imperceptibly.

3. Not long ... , at the G8 summit, world leaders agonized over a host of planetary problems, from global warming to the loss of biodiversity.

4. The volcano, with its slopes of pasture and forest, had been quiet for 400 years ... the last eruption, and 10,000 ... the last big one.

5. ... 1931, *Joy of Cooking* has guided home cooks through their struggles with roasting times, pie crusts and company dinners.

6. The disconsolate widow's been trying to drown her sorrows ... her husband passed away a fortnight ... .

2. Spot the possible mistakes and correct them. Write R for Right.

1. R / W............... Since Spain's Philip II has taken over Portugal in 1580, the Portuguese have nursed a deep fear of invasion.

2. R / W............... Since more than a decade climatologists had sounded the alarm: the continued release of "greenhouse gases" is warming the world.

3. R / W............... When the crisis has broken out more than two weeks ago, the United States opposed sending even food aid.

4. R / W............... Although she's been studying at Brown since three years, she didn't complete her doctorate yet.

5. R / W............... Since the days of Goya, who has painted many a bullfight, Spain's government regulated bull-fighting.

6. R / W............... They'd been searching for the wreck for ten years when the divers came across it by chance.

7. R / W............... Since 1800 food prices decreased by more than 90%. Who said we were a nation of whiners?

3. *It is* / *has been* / *was* + *since*. Put the verbs in brackets in the correct tense.

1. It is a long time since we last (have) .... dinner out.

2. It is two weeks that the same film (be) .... on at the Plaza.

3. It was several days since the refugees (have) .... anything to eat.

4. It is several decades since President Nixon (have) .... to resign.

5. It is the third time that voters (seem) .... to endorse power sharing.

6. It is 70 years since Britain's retail price index (RPI) first (publish) ....

Correction

1. **1**. Since - **2**. since / ago - **3**. ago - **4**. since / since - **5**. Since - **6**. since / ago ; a fortnight = 15 days

2. **1**. took over ; date (past tense) - **2**. For (a decade = ten years) / have been sounding - **3**. broke out ; past tense + ago - **4**. for three years (for + duration) / she hasn't completed (not yet) - **5**. who painted ; Goya is dead ; has regulated ; present perfect + since - **6**. R - **7**. have decreased ; since + 1800.

3. **1**. had - **2**. has been - **3**. had had - **4**. had - **5**. have seemed - **6**. was first published.

29 PAST / PRESENT (REVIEW) (1)

1. Spot the possible mistakes and correct them. Write R for Right.

1. R / W............... The waves gently broke and the sun has slowly set as we walk along the shore hand in hand.

2. R / W............... The original Globe theatre has burned down in 1613 and has been rebuilt, only to be closed in 1642 by Cromwell's Puritan government, and later dismantled.

3. R / W............... Since 1961, the population of the world almost doubled. As a result, food production per head had risen by 20% since 1961.

4. R / W............... Since 1976, when a Supreme Court opinion has paved the way for more executions, support for the death penalty is growing. Today over 70% of Americans tell opinion pollsters that they are favoring capital punishment.

5. R / W............... They spend the Easter weekend in Burgundy. They are going there twice a year. They had gone there over the past three years.

2. Put the verbs in the correct form (past / present perfect).

1. For 250 years, the men that (join) .... America's armed forces (measure) .... A current conundrum is that the average height of Americans (not increase) .... since the early 1970s, when men (reach) .... 177 cm. Europeans, on the other hand, (go) .... on growing. **2**. Over the past eight years the economy (expand) .... by almost 8% a year, while inflation (bring) .... down from 27% to 6%. **3**. Since the dictatorship (come) .... to an end in 1990, the country also (appear) .... to offer a model of political concord. **4**. The Great Red Spot of Jupiter (be) .... a puzzle since 1664, when Robert Hooke first (glimpse) .... it in his telescope. **5**. Ever since a coffee boom over a century ago (bring) .... money and migrants to Sao Paulo, Brazilians (see) .... the city as the locomotive of economic growth. **6**. Since 1945, there (be) .... around 100 serious armed conflicts in the world. In the past decade alone, conflicts (involve) .... large-scale murder or mistreatment of civilians and atrocities. **7**. For more than 60 years, ever since its young men (die) .... by the tens of thousands to end a war in Europe, the United States (champion) .... the cause of greater European unity. **8**. The gap between the richest and the poorest countries (widen) .... dramatically during the past century. **9**. The price of solar energy (fall) .... by half in every decade for the past 30 years, and (appear) .... likely to do so into the future.

Correction

1. **1**. were gently breaking / was slowly setting / walked - **2**. burned / was rebuilt - **3**. has almost doubled / has risen - **4**. paved / has grown / favor - **5**. are spending / go / have gone

2. **1**. joined / have been measured / has not increased / reached / have gone - **2**. has expanded / has been brought - **3**. came / has appeared - **4**. has been / glimpsed - **5**. brought / have seen - **6**. have been / have involved - **7**. died / has championed - **8**. has widened - **9**. has fallen / appears

30 PAST / PRESENT (REVIEW) (2)

Circle the letter of the correct answer.

1. It was the first time he ... such a detailed account of the riots.
a) reads b) is reading c) read d) had read

2. The ten warmest years ... 1860, when weather records ... first kept, all ... since 1980.
a) for / have / had occurred b) after / had / occurred
c) since / were / have occurred d) for / were / had occurred

3. Since the death of the rock star who ... himself a few weeks ago, the music press ... with letters from teenagers claiming to share his despair.
a) has shot / has flooded b) shot / has been flooded
c) was shot / was flooded d) has been shot / has been flooded

4. In the arid environment of southern Utah, residents ... to wrest a living ever since Brigham Young ... Mormons south from Salt Lake City to settle the area in the 19th century.
a) had been struggling / has sent b) have been struggling / sent
c) struggled / sent d) were struggling / have sent

5. ... American popular music ... with sex and violence in graphic ways.
a) Since years / are dealing b) In years / have been dealing
c) Years ago / were dealt d) For years / has dealt

6. On the eve of the trial, theories ... that the government ... up a massive sting operation that went terribly awry.
a) abound / is covering b) are abounding / cover
c) have been abounding / covers d) was abounding / covered

7. "Don't pay any attention," said the child's mother to her friend. "He ... a silly boy."
a) is acting b) becomes c) is being d) gets

8. They ... for several days before they finally ... the summit.
a) were climbing / have reached b) climbed / were reaching
c) had been climbing / reached d) will be climbing / will reach

9. Typhus ... Tom Paine just before he arrived in America, in 1774.
a) fell b) felled c) befell on d) fallen

10. "Would you like some more cookies?" "No, thanks ... enough."
a) I have been having b) I took already
c) I did take d) I've had

11. Now that the police ... the neighbors will stop quarrelling, I hope.
a) have come b) comes c) will come d) is coming

12. You know, it's really funny: I ... of you when the telephone rang and it was you.
a) had just a thought b) was just thinking
c) just think d) have just been thinking

Correction

1d ; it was the first / second time + past perfect - **2c** ; since + date ; when + past tense ; since + present perfect = from then till now - **3b** ; ago + past tense ; since + present perfect = from then till now - **4b** - **5d** - **6a** - **7c** - **8c** - **9c** - **10d** - **11a** - **12b**

31 PAST / PRESENT (REVIEW) (3)

Circle the letter of the correct answer.

1. She ... on her dissertation for 5 years and will be defending soon.
a) 's been working b) is working
c) works d) has worked

2. Mike, stop it! You ... a fool now.
a) are b) have been being
c) are being d) are to be not

3. For two generations now, members of my family ... lawyers.
a) are b) are being c) were d) have been

4. The trans-Neptunian object 2008 KV42 ... only this century.
a) was discovered b) has discovered
c) discovered d) it was discovered

5. "Have you ever visited Croatia?" - "Yes, I ... there last year."
a) was going b) have been
c) have been going d) went

6. We'd rather you ... town until the investigation is over.
a) didn't leave b) shouldn't leave
c) won't leave d) aren't to leave

7. The Chicago Bulls often ... in this gymnasium. I see them regularly.
a) are practicing b) practice
c) are used to practice d) practiced

8. When I ... a boy, I ... three miles to school every day.
a) have been / had walked b) was / walked
c) had been / was walking d) am / have walked

9. The surgeon took off the plaster he ... on 6 weeks before.
a) had put on b) put on
c) was putting on d) have put on

10. By the time he got to the theater the play ... .
a) has started already b) already started
c) had already started d) already was starting

11. Astronomers ... giant planets orbiting other stars. Now they ... the techniques needed to detect little ones.
a) have already discovered / are developing
b) already discovered / developed
c) had already discovered / have been developing
d) are already discovering / develop

12. "Have you managed to get in touch with Jim yet?" "No. I ... all day, but there is no answer, I'm afraid."
a) am calling b) called c) have been calling d) call

Correction

1a - **2c** ; do not confuse *you are being a fool* ÷ *you are a fool* - **3d** ; for + present perfect - **4a** - **5d** ; past action (last year) - **6a** ; past modal with *I'd rather + you / they, etc.* - **7b** ; present habit - **8b** - **9a** ; past perfect - **10c** - **11a** - **12c**

32 SHALL / WILL

1. Spot the mistakes and correct them. Write R for Right.

1. R / W............... How long shall your friends stay with us?
2. R / W............... If he won't fix the car, I'll have to do it myself.
3. R / W............... Shall you have tea or coffee?
4. R / W............... Shall you have time to go to the bank before it closes?
5. R / W............... He will be sixty next week.
6. R / W............... It's a secret. Promise me you don't tell anybody.
7. R / W............... If you ever go to Quebec, you are going to hear people speaking with a strange French accent.
8. R / W............... If you won't come with me, I am knowing that you are not my friend.
9. R / W............... Look at those dark clouds. It'll rain.
10. R / W............... Do you think the car of the future will run on hydrogen?
11. R / W............... If you will wait here a moment, I will fetch a chair.
12. R / W............... Nobody shall leave the premises until the thief owns up.
13. R / W............... You shall probably encounter some heavy seas when you round the Cape.
14. R / W............... Applicants shall provide a proof of residence to be eligible to qualify for a job with the US Treasury.
15. R / W............... Each party shall give one month's notice in writing in the event of termination.
16. R / W............... Don't worry, it will be done on time.

2. Complete the sentences using *shall, will, won't* or *shan't.*

1. I'll see you next week, ... I? **2**. That will be the doctor, ...it? **3**. I feel thirsty. .... we have a drink? **4**. He .... play for hours, if you let him, ...he? **5**. It says in the Bible that the last .... be the first. **6**. The car .... start if you push it, ... it? **7**. What hotel .... we be staying at? How long .... we be staying? **8**. I think the lecture .... be interesting. **9**. I suppose Professor Jones .... talk about phonetics? **10**. .... you lend me your car to go shopping? No, I .... You .... just have to take the bus or go on foot. **11**. I've got to stay in bed. I .... be able to get up for three weeks. **12**. You .... have your book tomorrow. I .... bring it back as early as possible. **13**. "............ you have port or brandy?" "I .... have some port, please." **14**. .... you be ready in, say, five minutes? **15**. .... you drive please? I can't see very well at night.

Correction

1. **1**. will - **2**. R - **3**. Will - **4**. Will - **5**. R - **6**. won't - **7**. will - **8**. I'll know - **9**. it's going to rain - **10**. R - **11**. R - **12**. will (US) also possible - **13**. will - **14**. R - **15**. R - **16**. R

2. **1**. shall - **2**. won't - **3**. shall - **4**. 'll / won't - **5**. shall - **6**. will / won't - **7**. shall / shall - **8**. will - **9**. will - **10**. Will / won't / 'll - **11**. shan't - **12**. shall / 'll - **13**. will / will - **14**. Will - **15**. Will

33 FUTURE (WILL / PRESENT SIMPLE / PRESENT CONTINUOUS)

1. Choose the correct tense (present simple / continuous, *will*).

1. The G8 heads of state and government (meet) .... in Denver in July.
2. We (go) .... home before it (get) .... dark.
3. Where you girls (have) .... lunch today?
4. We (have) .... a dinner tonight. Afterwards we (go) .... to a charity concert.
5. Just bear with me. We (go out) .... for lunch as soon as the meeting (be) .... over.
6. I (buy) .... her a new iPod for Christmas.
7. I see that *Batman* (come) .... to our local cinema next week. Oh good. We (go) .... and see it together on Friday night then?
8. I (be) .... promoted next month. The assistant manager (leave) .... and I (take) .... over the department.
9. Hurry up. The shuttle (leave) .... in just a few minutes.
10. What time school (break up) .... tomorrow?

2. Combine the numbered elements with the lettered ones.

1. Which project are you going to work on next?
2. Look at those dark clouds!
3. I'd better run. I'm already late as it is.
4. Are you free this weekend?
5. How's your research going?
6. Are you flying home?
7. When will you be there?
8. I'm giving a party Saturday. Are you coming?

a. .... Looks like it's going to rain any minute.
b. .... Great. My paper has been accepted and I'm going to a conference in San Diego in July.
c. .... Tomorrow. My plane lands at 21:00.
d. .... I haven't decided for sure. Probably a nano device able to detect low concentrations of chemical agents.
e. .... We'll see you later then.
f. .... Sorry, I have too much work.
g. .... No, I'm visiting an aunt in Brussels.
h. .... No, I'm taking the high speed train.

Correction

1. **1**. are meeting - **2**. 'll go / it gets - **3**. are you girls having - **4**. 're having / 're going - **5**. 'll go / is over - **6**. 'll buy / 'm going to buy - **7**. is coming / Shall we go - **8**. 'm being promoted / is leaving / 'm taking over - **9**. leaves - **10**. does school break up

2. a2 - b5 - c7 - d1 - e3 - f8 - g4 - h6

34 FUTURE CONTINUOUS

1. This is the US President's diary. Imagine what next week holds and make sentences using the *future continuous*.

1. Tomorrow at 8, he (have breakfast with the vice-president / hand out medals to deserving veterans / work in the Oval Office).

....

2. In the evening, he (attend a cocktail party / go to a fund-raiser / meet Congress representatives / watch a movie with the family).

....

3. On Tuesday, he (have lunch with the FEMA authorities / tour flood-stricken areas in the Midwest).

....

4. On Wednesday, he (chair a Cabinet meeting / give a commencement address at Yale / entertain foreign dignitaries at dinner).

....

5. On Thursday, he (fly to Madrid for a NATO summit / meet Britain's prime minister for lunch / stop over in Brussels for talks with high-level Europeans).

....

6. On Friday, he (meet with the French President / play golf with Tiger Woods / attend a gala evening at the Paris Opera House).

....

7. On Saturday, he (fly to Camp David with a few friends / jog in the morning / relax in the afternoon / catch up on his reading).

....

8. On Sunday, he (preach in a D.C. Baptist Church / have a few Democratic senators for brunch / prepare for his meeting with the Russian president).

....

2. Put the verbs in the present future or continuous future.

1. What you (have) .... to drink? Orange juice or something stronger? **2**. I hope you win this tournament. I (think) .... of you. **3**. You (recognize) .... him fairly easily. He (wear) .... a red cap with Red Sox written on it. **4**. He's been promoted manager of the company. He (work) .... directly under the chairman's orders. **5**. Experts estimate that by 2050, more than 1.5 billion people on the planet (speak) .... or (study) .... English. **6**. In the future, robots (perform) .... more and more tasks for men. **7**. I (know) .... my test results next week. **8**. The Mexicans (have) .... trouble getting across the Rio Grande. The Border Patrol (watch) .... out for them.

Correction

1. **1**. he will be having / will be handing / will be working - **2**. he will be attending / be going / will be meeting / will be watching - **3**. he will be having / will be touring - **4**. he will be chairing / will be giving / will be entertaining - **5**. he will be flying / will be meeting / will be stopping - **6**. he will be meeting / will be playing / will be attending - **7**. he will be flying / will be jogging / will be relaxing / will be catching up - **8**. he will be preaching / will be having / will be preparing

2. **1**. will you have - **2**. 'll be thinking - **3**. 'll recognize / 'll be wearing - **4**. 'll be working - **5**. will be speaking / studying - **6**. will be performing - **7**. 'll know - **8**. will have / will be watching

35 FUTURE PERFECT SIMPLE / CONTINUOUS

1. Spot the possible mistakes and correct them. Write R for Right.

1. R / W............... By October, he will have started his 5th year in teaching.
2. R / W............... The first act will started by the time we get to the Met.
3. R / W............... I hope you will forget this incident by tomorrow.
4. R / W............... I expect it will have snowed by the time the Christmas holidays start.
5. R / W............... In 2014, it will be 70 years since the Allied Forces landed in Normandy.
6. R / W............... By the time it closes, two million people will see the Stella exhibition.

2. Put the verbs in brackets in the correct tense.

1. Before you have a chance to see them live, all the concerts (be / sell out) .... **2**. By the end of the year, he (fly) .... more than a million miles. **3**. I (finish) .... this exercise long before you get back. **4**. If we don't get to the party before 6, they (eat) .... all the appetizers. **5**. By 2020, China (displace) .... the US as the world's leading producer of greenhouse gases.

3. Write T (True) or F (False) for the statement that follows each numbered sentence.

1. By this time tomorrow, she will have been operated on.
She hasn't been operated on : ......

2. I'll have finished the shopping by the time you get home.
I will be shopping when you get home : ......

3. By the end of the year, he will have been working for the *Times* for 15 years.
He started working for the *Times* for more than 15 years : ......

4. Our activities will have been outsourced by the end of next year.
They will outsource their activities in two years' time : ......

5. I will have finished marking the test papers by tonight.
I will finish marking tonight : ......

6. By the time we get home, we will have visited 35 countries.
They haven't got home yet : ......

Correction

1. **1**. R - **2**. will have started - **3**. will have forgotten - **4**. R - **5**. will have been - **6**. will have seen

2. **1**. will have been sold out - **2**. will have flown - **3**. will have finished - **4**. will have eaten - **5**. will have displaced

3. 1T - 2F - 3F - 4F - 5T - 6T

36 BE GOING TO

1. Complete the sentences with the correct form of the verb (*present continuous, will, be going to*).

1. It may well be that in the future people (spend) .... their holidays on Mars.
2. Who (look) .... after Grandma when we go on holiday?
3. Professor Krugman (arrive) .... tomorrow. He (spend) .... the weekend and (give) .... a lecture on Monday.
4. You (look) .... for a job or (take) .... a vacation once you've sat your exams?
5. You're quite clever for your age. You (be) .... a Nobel prize-winner like your father when you grow up?
6. "Mr. Blair, why didn't you call little Leo Blair Tuscany—after all David Beckham called his son Brooklyn?" "I (not answer) .... such a rude question."
7. Next week, Mr. Smith almost certainly (be elected) .... the European Parliament's new president.
8. Where are all those children going? They (pick) .... blackberries. They (be) .... back by noon, then they probably (be) .... very sick.
9. If I've told you once I've told you a thousand times. You (not / stay up) .... tonight until all hours. I (not / tell) .... you again.
10. They (get married) .... when Robin graduates from college.

2. Circle the letter of the correct answer.

1. I have no money left. a) Don't worry I'll lend you some. b) I'm going to lend you some. c) I'm lending you some.	**2.** Sorry, I forgot to post the parcel but a) I'll do it now. b) I'm going to do it now. c) I doing it.
3. Hamilton has taken the lead. I think a) he wins. b) he will win. c) he is going to win.	**4.** I think Betty a) is going to like your present. b) will like your present. c) is liking your present.
5. "I have a splitting headache." "Wait here, a) I'll get some aspirin for you." b) I shall get you some aspirin." c) I'm getting some aspirin."	**6.** If you decide to take up Chinese, a) I'm going to be your teacher. b) I'll be your teacher. c) I'm being your teacher.

Correction

1. **1**. will spend - **2**.'s going to look - **3**. is arriving / 's spending / giving - **4**. Are you going to look / take - **5**. Are you going to be - **6**. 'm not going to answer - **7**. will almost certainly be elected - **8**. are going to pick / will be back / are probably going to be - **9**. 're not going to stay / 'm not going to tell - **10**. will get married

2. 1a - 2a - 3c - 4a/b - 5a/b - 6b

37 BE TO

1. Indicate whether the 'be to' actions have actually taken place (A) or not (B).

1. What am I to do if I get lost? ....
2. They are to arrive late tonight. ....
3. Chernobyl was to be shut down after the accident. ....
4. No bicycle is to be left on these grounds. ....
5. He was to be assassinated in 1968. ....
6. You are not to play with matches again. ....
7. The senator was to have been operated on. ....
8. Ophelia, who was to play the part, collapsed with nervous exhaustion. ....

2. Indicate which idea is expressed in each sentence: *decision • destiny • obligation • project • order.*

1. Their daughter is to be married soon. ....
2. You are to keep the plan secret. ....
3. President Nixon was to resign in 1974. ....
4. The Personnel Manager told Priscilla that she was to be his new assistant. ....
5. After playing a decisive role in the peace negotiations he was to be awarded the Nobel Prize for Peace. ....
6. The president is to deliver a major speech on foreign policy. ....
7. The author went to live in Canada where he was to write two novels before his death. ....
8. Six-year old Tommy was told not to play with the plug. ....
9. That perfidious friend of yours is to be shunned. ....
10. The children are not to be left without supervision. ....

3. Combine the numbered elements with the lettered ones.

1. He knew he had made a mistake by appointing him to the board. ...
2. If ever she were to have an accident, ...
3. You are not to go out without my permission, ...
4. The book is to be returned ...
5. The prisoner was to have been handed to the authorities ...

a. she said I was to open the envelope. **b**. to the library by the end of the month. **c**. He was later to regret his decision. **d**. when he escaped. **e**. is that understood?

Correction

1. 1B - 2B - 3A - 4B - 5A - 6A - 7B - 8B

2. **1**. project - **2**. order - **3**. destiny - **4**. decision - **5**. destiny - **6**. project - **7**. destiny - **8**. order - **9**. order - **10**. order

3. 1c - 2a - 3e - 4b - 5d

38 TIME CLAUSES (1)

Circle the letter of the right answer.

1. By the time a plane ..., its fuel tanks are nearly empty.
a) has been landing b) will land
c) will have landed d) lands

2. She said she didn't have a clue as to when she ... .
a) would arrive b) has arrived c) will arrive d) arrives

3. Will you miss me when I ...?
a) will go b) am gone c) will have you d) went

4. We shall leave as soon as you ... packing.
a) are finishing b) finished
c) have finished d) will have finished

5. After you ... that thriller will you lend it to me?
a) have finished b) will finish
c) will have finished d) are finishing

6. Brian said he would send us an SMS as soon as he ... .
a) would have arrived b) would arrive
c) has arrived d) had arrived

7. He said he ... travel round the world when he ... rich
a) would / will be b) will / was
c) would / was d) would / would be

8. The day will come ... China ... a decisive role in world politics.
a) that / plays b) where / will play
c) when / will play d) ø / plays

9. He'll look for a job when he ... school.
a) left b) will have left c) will leave d) leaves

10. Until she ... a job, she'll stay home.
a) will get b) gets c) will have got d) is getting

11. They will be granted political asylum as soon as they ... evidence that their lives would be at risk if they returned to their home country.
a) are producing b) will be producing
c) have produced d) will have produced

12. Don't cross the street ... the green light.
a) a long as b) until c) as soon as d) while

13. The civil war will go on ... factions cease sowing hatred.
a) unless b) providing c) in case d) once

14. He will join up with the national squad ... he comes through unscathed from his club's match against Worcester.
a) until b) once c) provided d) in case

Correction

1d - 2a - 3b - 4c - 5a - 6d - 7c - 8c - 9d - 10b - 11c - 12b - 13a - 14c

39 TIME CLAUSES (2)

1. Spot the possible mistakes and correct them. Write R for Right.

1. R / W............... The prisoner won't talk until he would see a lawyer.
2. R / W............... She'll be delighted when she will hear the news.
3. R / W............... As soon as I am setting up my own firm, I'll start hiring.
4. R / W............... The electricity will remain cut off till you paid the bill.
5. R / W............... The bank said it would lend me the money as soon as I needed it.
6. R / W............... I would have hired you once you will become certified.
7. R / W............... He'd probably have applied for Caltech after he graduated from high school.
8. R / W............... He knew he would feel relieved as soon as the operation had been carried out.
9. R / W............... For as long as stricter laws do not pass, the funding of political campaigns will remain controversial.
10. R / W............... She knew that, as soon as the shelling stops, she would be able to leave her home and fetch some water.

2. Put the verbs in the correct tense.

1. The pub will remain closed for as long as the health inspectors (not declare) .... it safe to eat there. **2**. The weary traveling salesman will not go home as long as he (get) .... some encyclopedias left to sell. **3**. You won't be allowed to leave the country until the authorities (return) .... your passport. **4**. Once you (sign) .... the contract, the agent will hand you the keys to your new house. **5**. The jury will not return their verdict until they (reach) .... a decision.

3. Complete the sentences using *after / as soon as / before / by the end / by the time / once / till / until / when / while.*

1. .... of summer, I will have completed my thesis.
2. We won't make any decision .... the boss has arrived.
3. If we don't hurry, night will have fallen .... we reach the valley.
4. .... you have had a glass of milk, you will feel much better.
5. I will lock all the doors .... the last guest has gone home.
6. .... as Rob gets a promotion, they'll be able to move to a larger flat.
7. She'll get a new car .... she graduates.
8. I will look after the baby .... you go shopping.
9. Students from middle-income families are loaded down with heavy debt .... they earn a diploma.

Correction

1. **1**. he's seen - **2**. she hears - **3**. I have set up - **4**. you have paid - **5**. R - **6**. you had become - **7**. he had graduated - **8**. R - **9**. laws have not been passed - **10**. the shelling stopped

2. **1**. have not declared - **2**. has got - **3**. have returned - **4**. have signed - **5**. have reached

3. **1**. By the end - **2**. till / until - **3**. before - **4**. Once - **5**. after - **6**. As soon as - **7**. when - **8**. while - **9**. by the time

40 FUTURE (REVIEW)

1. Spot the possible mistakes and correct them. Write R for Right.

1. R / W............... I will call you when I got your letter.
2. R / W............... "What's wrong with your car?" "It is not starting."
3. R / W............... It is taking three days' climbing for the expedition to reach the summit of Everest.
4. R / W............... Next Tuesday, the Americans are going to the polls to elect a new president.
5. R / W............... They're thinking of going to Greece for the next summer holidays.
6. R / W............... By 2020, the Internet as we know it today will probably change out of all recognition.
7. R / W............... Hook children on a brand today, and with any luck they will still be using it twenty years later.
8. R / W............... I throw a big party for my 50th birthday.

2. Choose the correct form of the verb to indicate future events.

1. (Someone's knocking at the door). Don't get up, my daughter (go and find out) who it is. ....
2. "It's another beggar. I (tell) him to get lost?" ....
3. "When you (order)?" "As soon as I've read the menu."
....
4. What you (do) if you can't find your passport? ....
5. "What you (do) this Sunday?" ....
6. "How you (pay)? Cash or charge?" ....
7. Go and see a good movie, it (take) your mind off your worries.
....
8. Call me around three, I (work) probably in my study.
....
9. I can't see you tonight, I (take) my wife to the opera.
....

3. Rewrite sentences using elements in brackets.

1. Will you have some more turkey? (**like**) ....
2. Max will be promoted soon. (**be to**) ....
3. We won't go to the lecture. (**choose**) ....
4. I'll be going to my nephew's for the weekend. (**intend**) ....
5. He'll be leaving soon. (**be about to**) ....
6. He won't accept your apology. (**refuse**) ....

Correction

1. **1**. was going to call - **2**. won't start - **3**. will take - **4**. will be going - **5**. R - **6**. will probably have changed - **7**. R - **8**. I'll be throwing / I'm going to throw

2. **1**. will go and find out - **2**. Shall I tell - **3**. "When are you going to order?" - **4**. What will you do - **5**. What are you doing - **6**. How are you paying / are you going to pay? - **7**. will take - **8**. will probably be working - **9**. 'm taking

3. **1**. Would you like some more turkey? **2**. Max is to be promoted soon. **3**. We have chosen not to go. **4**. I intend to go to my nephew's for the weekend. **5**. He's about to leave. **6**. He refuses to accept your apology.

41 PRESENT CONDITIONAL

1. Spot the possible mistakes and correct them. Write R for Right.

1. R / W............... If the rain didn't let up, the rivers are likely to burst their banks and the whole area will be flooded.
2. R / W............... If I had a green card, I can work in the USA.
3. R / W............... If you finish with the paper, I'd like to borrow it, please.
4. R / W............... If I went to Hawaii, I have a one-day stopover in Los Angeles.
5. R / W............... If the authorities don't curb pollution in downtown Athens, monuments will be damaged even further by exhaust fumes.
6. R / W............... If he retires at 55 he wouldn't get a full pension.
7. R / W............... If you vote for him, you will not have regretted it.
8. R / W............... I would buy that computer if it was cheaper.

2. Combine the numbered elements with the lettered ones.

1. If he drops out at such an early age	**a.** I'm sure she'd listen.
2. If you take him to court	**b.** unless you train harder.
3. If the weather holds	**c.** you'll be able to get him to pay alimony.
4. Suppose you talked to her	**d.** the launch will proceed on time.
5. You won't make much progress	**e.** he'll never find a decent job.

3. Put the verbs in brackets in the correct tense.

1. Apparently, if you take an aspirin every day it (reduce) .... the risk of heart disease.
2. The US President has threatened to veto the new bill on welfare reform the Democrats (vote) .... it.
3. He (break off) .... diplomatic relations with those countries which do not respect human rights.
4. He (not speak) .... Russian unless you force him to.
5. If the firefighters don't get here soon the warehouse (burn) .... down by noon.
6. If you put your glasses on, you (can / see) .... the film and read the subtitles.
7. If you run into problems, you always (can / ask) .... your father to help you out.

Correction

1. **1**. doesn't let up - **2**. I would be able to work - **3**. you have finished - **4**. I go - **5**. R - **6**. he retired - **7**. you won't regret - **8**. you were ; *was* is often heard but is used incorrectly

2. 1e - 2c - 3d - 4a - 5b

3. **1**. reduces - **2**. should the Democrats vote - **3**. will break off - **4**. won't speak - **5**. will have burnt down - **6**. you could (if *put* is in the past tense) / you'll be able (if *put* is in the present tense) - **7**. you can / could always ask

42 PAST CONDITIONAL

1. Complete the sentences with elements in brackets.

1. Suppose Bell hadn't invented the telephone,
➪ (someone else / have)

....

2. Nelson wouldn't have made such an easy target for French snipers,
➪ (if / he / not insist / on wearing his medals)

....

3. The Spanish Armada might have succeeded in invading England,
➪ (if / God / be on the side of the English / in 1588)

....

4. If Cleopatra's nose had been shorter,
➪ (the whole face of the earth / change) *(Pascal)*

....

2. Combine the numbered elements with the lettered ones.

1. If the climbers had retraced their steps when the storm broke out,
2. If the investigators had not acted swiftly,
3. If she had exercised,
4. If she hadn't been chatting away on the mobile phone,
5. If we had had a map,

a. ...... she wouldn't have put on so much weight.
b. ...... we wouldn't have got lost.
c. ...... they would be alive today.
d. ...... the accident wouldn't have happened.
e. ...... the kidnappers would have killed their hostage.

3. Rewrite sentences in the past conditional using *if.*

1. He never went to Britain or the USA. How could he be expected to improve his English?

....

2. He never combed his hair or had a shave. That's why he looked so scruffy.

....

3. The reactor ought to have been sealed. Radiation kept on leaking out.

....

4. He failed to complete his Ph.D. in time. He was not offered the job.

....

Correction

1. **1**. ...somebody else would have. **2**. If Nelson hadn't insisted on wearing his medals, he wouldn't have made such an easy target for French snipers. **3**. If God hadn't been on the side of the English in 1588, the Spanish Armada might have succeeded in invading England. **4**. ...the whole face of the Earth would have been changed

2. 1c - 2e - 3a - 4d - 5b

3. **1**. Had he gone / If he had gone to... he would have improved his English. **2**. Had he combed / If he had combed his hair / he had had a shave, he wouldn't have looked so scruffy. **3**. Had the reactor been sealed / If the reactor had been sealed, radiation would not have kept on leaking out. **4**. Had he completed / If he had completed his Ph.D. in time, he would have been offered the job.

43 CONDITIONALS (REVIEW)

1. Spot the possible mistakes and correct them. Write R for Right.

1. R / W............... The accountant would have gone to jail if I did not spot the mistake in the books.

2. R / W............... Had I known about his troubles I could help him.

3. R / W............... The economic crisis could hit much harder if Franklin Roosevelt had not taken the appropriate measures.

4. R / W............... If Europeans wanted to create more jobs, they will have to change the laws that make it expensive to employ people.

5. R / W............... Even if the Archduke Ferdinand hadn't been shot in Sarajevo, World War One would break out anyway.

6. R / W............... If I was you, I would buy bonds rather than shares.

2. Choose the correct form of the verb.

1. Suppose there was a fire in the Channel Tunnel? What (happen) .... to the passengers on the trains?

2. If you had arrived on time, you (not miss) .... your flight.

3. If you buy such a large house, you (pay) .... a high property tax.

4. If we had heeded the warnings of environmentalists twenty years ago, we (may / be able to / combat) .... pollution more efficiently.

5. Galileo (not prove) .... the earth goes round the sun, space flight would never have been possible.

6. If the ice age (not occur) .... the geography of today's world would be completely different.

3. Write T (True) or F (False) for the statement that follows each numbered sentence.

1. The computer firm will go bust if they don't find new sources of financing.
The firm is still doing business : ......

2. John to Steve : What would do if you won the jackpot?
Steve has become a millionaire : ......

3. Jack might have won the race if he had had better equipment.
Jack didn't have the upper hand : ......

4. If Matthew had had time he would have completed the report in time.
Matthew still has to finish it : ......

5. I would have recorded the movie had my DVD player not broken.
I could record the DVD : ......

Correction

1. **1**. had not spotted - **2**. I would have been able to help - **3**. would have hit - **4**. want - **5**. would have broken out - **6**. If I were you

2. **1**. would happen - **2**. wouldn't have missed - **3**. 'll pay - **4**. might have been able to combat - **5**. Had Galileo not proved - **6**. had not occurred

3. 1T - 2F - 3T - 4T - 5F

44 TENSES (REVIEW)

1. Spot the possible mistakes and correct them. Write R for Right.

1. R / W............... During the Great Depression of the 1930s, firms lay off workers, cut wages and abandoned their welfare programs. Union membership grows and, with the New Deal, government involvement in social welfare increased dramatically.

2. R / W............... For most Spaniards, 1898 was the year of "the disaster", when the country's last big colonies, the Philippines and Cuba, lost to the United States, and Spain started sliding into a long period of isolation and decline.

3. R / W............... For 50 years, relations froze between the United States and Cuba, the communist island 90 miles off its coast. It is the cold war's last redoubt.

4. R / W............... For generations rural Australians regarded land clearing as a God-given right. It is not one that will be given up easily.

5. R / W............... The United Nations conference on climate change in Kyoto in 1998 set targets to reduce the emission of greenhouse gases, such as carbon dioxide, which cause global warming.

6. R / W............... The question of when, and by whom, the Americas first populated exercised scholars since the idea that everyone now alive is descended from Noah has been rejected in the 19th century.

7. R / W............... This year it is 400 years since Spanish *conquistadores* first has claimed the land to the north of the Rio Grande. Spanish-speakers from the rest of the American continent never ceased to follow their example.

2. Put the verbs in brackets in the correct tense.

For at least the past 300 years, Britain (try) .... to prevent the emergence of a single dominant power on the continent of Europe. From 1700 to 1815, it (build) .... a succession of alliances to contain France. In the 20th century, it (use) .... balance-of-power politics to contain Germany. Despite the huge cost of two world wars, the policy (be) .... successful. Britain never (experience) .... defeat and occupation; indeed, the British (remember) .... the Second World War as, in Churchill's words, "their finest hour". And the rest of Europe (rescue) .... from one-power domination. Britain's reaction to the growth of the European Union deeply (influence) .... by this instinctive belief in the need to prevent the rise of a controlling power in Europe. Ever since it joined the EU, Britain's policy (characterise) .... by repeated and largely fruitless attempts to "break up the Franco-German alliance". (*The Economist*).

Correction

1. **1**. laid / grew - **2**. were lost - **3**. have been frozen - **4**. have regarded - **5**. R - **6**. were first populated has exercised / has been - **7**. claimed / have never ceased

2. For at least the past 300 years, Britain **has tried** to prevent the emergence of a single dominant power on the continent of Europe. From 1700 to 1815, it **built** a succession of alliances to contain France. In the 20th century, it **used** balance-of-power politics to contain Germany. Despite the huge cost of two world wars, the policy **was** successful. Britain never **experienced** defeat and occupation; indeed, the British **remember** the Second World War as, in Churchill's words, "their finest hour". And the rest of Europe **was rescued** from one-power domination. Britain's reaction to the growth of the European Union **has been** deeply **influenced** by this instinctive belief in the need to prevent the rise of a controlling power in Europe. Ever since it joined the EU, Britain's policy **has been characterised** by repeated and largely fruitless attempts to "break up the Franco-German alliance".

45 CAN / COULD / BE ABLE TO

1. Spot the possible mistakes and correct them. Write R for Right.

1. R / W............... She was able to be murdered by a spurned lover, who knows?
2. R / W............... She used to can speak Russian well.
3. R / W............... I ran as fast as I can and can just catch the bus.
4. R / W............... She hid so well that we can't have found her.
5. R / W............... When she was four, she is able to read quite well already.
6. R / W............... The police got suspicious when they found I had a gun, but I can convince them it was all above board.
7. R / W............... Could you walk or did they have to carry you?

2. Complete the sentences using *can / could / be able to.*

1. When we first went to Soviet Russia we (go) .... anywhere in safety and we (park) .... wherever we liked. **2**. When you start doing better at school you (watch) .... your silly soap operas on television. **3**. You (swim) ....? Yes, I ...., I (do) .... the backstroke and the crawl. I (swim) .... since the age of six. **4**. I was sitting a long way from the stage. I (hear) .... all right, but I (see) .... very well. **5**. When the flat tyre had been fixed, we (continue) .... on our journey. **6**. You (remember) .... what happened? I (not remember) .... who I am, let alone what happened. **7**. If any mail comes for me, you please (forward) .... it to this address? **8**. The boxer was so exhausted after going ten rounds that he (not / walk) .... and had to be carried out. **9**. If the *Mayflower* had sunk, that (change) .... the fate of America?

3. Circle the letter of the correct answer.

1. *Hier, j'ai pu faire du vélo.* a) I was able to ride my bike. b) I could ride my bike.	**2.** *Jadis on pouvait faire du vélo (en toute sécurité).* a) We could ride our bikes. b) We used to be able to ride our bikes.
3. *Tu pourrais y aller à vélo.* a) You could go by bike. b) You could've gone by bike.	**4.** *Tu pourras y aller en vélo.* a) You'll can go by bike. b) You'll be able to go by bike.
5. *Tu aurais pu y aller à vélo.* a) You could have gone by bike. b) You could go by bike.	**6.** *Il put y aller en vélo.* a) He is able to go by bike. b) He was able to go by bike.

Correction

1. **1**. could have been murdered - **2**. to be able to speak - **3**. could / could just catch - **4**. could not find - **5**. could read - **6**. I was able to convince them - **7**. Were you able to walk

2. **1**. could go / could park - **2**. 'll be able to watch - **3**. Can you swim? / can / can do / have been able to swim - **4**. could hear / couldn't see - **5**. were able to continue - **6**. Can you remember / can't remember - **7**. could you please forward - **8**. couldn't walk - **9**. could that have changed

3. 1a - 2b - 3a - 4b - 5a - 6b

46 COULD / COULD HAVE

1. Circle the letter of the correct answer.

1. *Tu pourrais te blesser.* a) You could have been hurt. b) You could get hurt.	**2.** *Tu aurais pu te blesser.* a) You could have got hurt. b) You could hurt.
3. *Il pouvait envoyer un texto.* a) He could send an SMS. b) He could have sent an SMS.	**4.** *Il aurait pu envoyer un texto.* a) He could send an SMS. b) He could have sent an SMS.
5. *Comment aurait-il pu savoir?* a) How could he know? b) How could he have known?	**6.** *Comment pouvait-il savoir ?* a) How could he know? b) How could he have known?
7. *Si j'avais pu y aller !* a) I wish I could go to there! b) I wish I could have gone there!	**8.** *Si seulement je savais y aller !* a) I wish I knew how to go there. b) I wish I can know how to go.
9. *Je n'entendais pas sa voix.* a) I couldn't have heard his voice. b) I couldn't hear his voice.	**10.** *Je n'aurais pas pu venir.* a) I couldn't have come. b) I couldn't come.

2. Complete the sentences using *can, could* or *could have.*

1. Many species (can / disappear) .... if man doesn't change his ways. **2**. He (can / be) .... in hospital for another week, according to what the doctors say. **3**. He said that this journalist sure (can ask) .... embarrassing questions! **4**. If you did come, you (can stay) .... as long as you wished. **5**. The Russians successfully (can / land) .... a space probe on Mars? It is highly unlikely. **6**. How he (can / tell) .... me such lies? **7**. He was traveling without id. He (can / arrest) ....

3. Write T (True) or F (False) for the statement that follows each numbered sentence.

1. Corporate Britain wish the government could do something about the high pound which is penalizing their exports.

The government has taken action : ......

2. Grandma couldn't have made it down the stairs all on her own.

Somebody may have helped her : ......

3. How could Adrian have squandered all his fortune in so short a time?

He's rich now : ......

4. I wish we could have booked a night crossing.

We could have slept on board : ......

Correction

1. 1b - 2a - 3a - 4b - 5b - 6a - 7b - 8a - 9b - 10a

2. **1**. could disappear - **2**. could be - **3**. can ask - **4**. could stay - **5**. Could the Russians have successfully landed - **6**. could he have told - **7**. could have been arrested

3. **1F** - **2T** - **3F** ; he's broke - **4T**

47 MAY / MIGHT

1. Spot the possible mistakes and correct them. Write R for Right.

1. R / W............... Malcolm must be lying when he spoke to you, but I'm not really certain.
2. R / W............... With all this fog, traveling by car may be dangerous.
3. R / W............... A peace treaty might have been be signed next month.
4. R / W............... What with last night's storm, the lines may bring down in the gale.
5. R / W............... They may not have realized that he is drowning.
6. R / W............... I may have not been here when you get back so we may as well said goodbye now.
7. R / W............... This may been the man who can help the police with their enquiries.

2. Rewrite sentences using *may / might*.

1. He didn't come to class yesterday. Perhaps he is ill.

....

2. I see him in the garden almost every day. It's quite possible he's retired.

....

3. I wonder if there was enough wind for him to fly his kite.

....

4. Throw me over the *TV Times*, could you? Perhaps there's a good film on television tonight.

....

5. Hamilton is going very slowly. I wonder what's wrong. It could be a slow puncture or overheating.

....

6. If you tell me when you arrive, perhaps I can manage to put you up.

....

3. Past (a), present (b) or future (c) action? Circle the right letter.

1. **(a) (b) (c)** He may be elected, who knows?
2. **(a) (b) (c)** With more funds, he might have been elected.
3. **(a) (b) (c)** They may be getting a divorce.
4. **(a) (b) (c)** We may give up this rat race and go and keep sheep in the Welsh Mountains.
5. **(a) (b) (c)** You might be able to survive on $5 a day, but knowing you I very much doubt it.
6. **(a) (b) (c)** She said she might have to cancel the meeting.

Correction

1. **1**. may have been lying - **2**. R - **3**. might be signed - **4**. may have been brought - **5**. was drowning - **6**. I may not be / we may as well say - **7**. may be

2. **1**. He may be ill. **2**. He may well have retired, I suppose. **3**. There may not have been enough wind for him to fly his kite. **4**. There may be a good film on television tonight. **5**. He may have a slow puncture or the car might be overheating. **6**. I may be able to put you up.

3. 1c - 2a - 3b - 4c - 5c - 6c

48 MUST / HAVE TO

1. Circle the letter of the correct answer.

1. You must salute an officer. a) They like it that way. b) It's the regulation.	**2.** He has to stay overnight. a) I've asked him to do so. b) He can't get home tonight.
3. You have to call her 'Madam'. a) She likes it that way. b) That's the regulation address.	**4.** We'll have to eat early. a) Otherwise we won't get there before nightfall. b) That's the time arranged.
5. You must take off your shoes if you want to come in. a) They are all worn out. b) I won't have you leaving muddy footsteps all over the carpet.	**6.** He'll have to move the car by himself. a) I shan't help him. b) Poor chap; he's got no one to help him.
7. He must come no matter what he thinks. a) He's likely to come. b) I demand that he come.	**8.** There must be a mistake! a) I'm sure there is one b) There's likely to be one
9. Oh, you must come and visit us this summer. a) You don't have much choice. b) That would be so nice.	**10.** She can come if she must. a) The idea doesn't appeal to me though. b) Although the idea doesn't appeal to her.

2. Complete the sentences using *must* or *have to*.

1. French children (stay) .... on at school till the age of 16. **2**. All the flights were booked up. I (go) .... by train. **3**. He said his mother had always told him he .... (beware) of strangers. **4**. You (put out) .... your cigarette before entering the Paris metro. **5**. I (wear) .... a jacket and a tie for the job interview if I want to be taken seriously. **6**. He (miss) .... his connection because I don't see his name on the passenger list.

3. Spot the possible mistakes and correct them. Write R for Right.

1. R / W............... Have we to do as we're told?

2. R / W............... It was so cold in June that they must switch the heating on.

3. R / W............... I've filled the tank up. You haven't to worry.

4. R / W............... "Madam, you mustn't park here. It's forbidden."

5. R / W............... You don't have to forget to leave me the access code, otherwise I shan't be able to get in.

Correction

1. 1b - 2b - 3b - 4a - 5b - 6a/b - 7b - 8a - 9b - 10a

2. **1**. have to stay ; *rappel : la nécessité ou l'obligation peut avoir comme origine soit l'énonciateur, soit un état de fait, un règlement, des habitudes, etc. Dans le premier cas, on utilise* must, *dans le second* have to. *Cette règle n'est pas absolue.* - **2**. had to go - **3**. must beware ; *utilisation de must dans une proposition subordonnée de style indirect au passé. C'est le seul cas où* must *est possible au passé.* - **4**. have to put out - **5**. must / have to - **6**. must have missed

3. **1**. Do we have to do - **2**. they had to switch - **3**. You don't have to worry - **4**. R - **5**. You mustn't forget

49 MUST / MUSTN'T / NEEDN'T

1. Match each result with its direct cause.

Result	*Cause*
1. You needn't lock the door,	**a.** I can eat it cold.
2. You must book before twelve	**b.** there are plenty of seats
3. You must make a backup of your hard disk	**c.** I could have given you a ride.
4. You needn't send for information	**d.** you'll find everything you need on the Internet.
5. You needn't reheat the pie.	**e.** or there won't be any seats left.
6. You needn't book early	**f.** or you might lose files.
7. You needn't have taken the bus,	**g.** it's a safe neighborhood.

2. Put the verbs in the past tense.

1. We needn't go to the lecture if you don't feel like it.

....

2. The students don't have to type their papers.

....

3. I must leave now, but you needn't.

....

4. He must pay more than we do.

....

5. You don't need to carry such a heavy backpack.

....

3. Choose the correct form of the modal (*must / have to / need*).

1. They said South Africa was a beautiful country and that we .... go there on holiday.
2. You .... bring your tennis racket, we won't have time for a game.
3. You .... vote in the USA if you don't want to.
4. You .... call me every week, is that understood?
5. I'll give you a key so you .... ring the bell.
6. I .... go shopping today, there's plenty of food in the house.
7. I must leave now, but you .... You can stay as long as you want.
8. The law says I .... have my picture taken to get a new identity card.
9. They .... take a written test last year. Now it's compulsory.
10. Thank God I .... pay a lot of taxes this year.
11. You .... go to the bank. I can do it for you if you want.

Correction

1. 1g - 2e - 3f - 4d - 5a - 6b - 7c

2. **1**. We didn't have to go if you didn't feel like it. **2**. The students didn't need to / didn't have to type their papers. **3**. I had to / you didn't have to leave. **4**. He had to pay more than we did. **5**. You didn't have to carry / didn't need to carry... .

3. **1**. must - **2**. needn't - **3**. needn't - **4**. must - **5**. won't need to - **6**. don't need to / needn't go - **7**. needn't - **8**. must - **9**. didn't need to - **10**. haven't had to (present perfect) - **11**. don't have to

50 MUST / CAN'T

1. Combine the numbered elements with the lettered ones.

1. She's going to be a mother. **2.** I must have left my scarf in the restaurant. **3.** He's one of the main shareholders. **4.** The missing child is only 4. **5.** It only took you 10 minutes? **6.** You can't have invited John and Melissa!	**a.** He must be rolling in it. **b.** They hate each other's guts. **c.** She must be happy. **d.** You must have driven like the clappers. **e.** I can't find it anywhere. **f.** He can't have run away.

2. Circle the letter of the correct answer.

1. He ... suicide. He loved life too much for that.
a) must have committed b) can't have committed

2. They live in a penthouse on Fifth Avenue. It ... them an arm and a leg.
a) it must have cost b) it can't cost

3. The doctors ... on him where he lay, given the seriousness of his injuries.
a) can't have operated b) must have operated

4. Motorway traffic ... very heavy for the bank-holiday week end!
a) can have been b) must have been

5. He ... his pocket calculator the day he took his A-levels, surely?
a) can't have forgotten b) must have forgotten

6. He was not on board the 11 o'clock flight. He ... the next one.
a) can't have taken b) must have taken

3. Complete the sentences using *must* / *can't* (+ *have*) / *couldn't* (+ *have*).

1. I wonder who was making all that noise last night. It (be) .... the neighbors, they're away on vacation. **2**. I had my glasses when I left the classroom, so I (leave) .... them there. **3**. You (meet) .... her in Durham. She was staying with me. **4**. I tried to call your office this morning around 12, but got no answer. Your secretary (be) .... out for lunch. **5**. The van (swerve) .... to avoid hitting a deer. **6**. Even if I had had more time, I (never / complete) .... the project on time for tomorrow. **7**. If you can't even remember it, it (be) .... that important, right? **8**. Hip hop (be born) .... in a building designed by Frank Lloyd Wright or Mies van der Rohe.

Correction

1. 1c - 2e - 3a - 4f - 5d - 6b

2. 1b - 2a - 3b - 4b - 5a - 6b

3. **1**. can't have been - **2**. can't have left - **3**. can't have met - **4**. must have been - **5**. must have swerved - **6**. could never have completed - **7**. can't have been - **8**. couldn't have been born

51 DIDN'T NEED TO / NEEDN'T HAVE

1. Match each result with its direct cause.

Cause	Result
1. My tea was already sweetened **2.** I didn't need to buy a new car **3.** We needn't have waited for her, **4.** I didn't need to go by sea **5.** I didn't need to pay for it, **6.** You needn't have told him to his face.	**a.** because she never turned up. **b.** You could have written him a letter. **c.** I needn't have put any sugar in it. But I did, and it was undrinkable. **d.** because it was put on my father's account. **e.** my folks gave me their old one. **f.** but flying would have cost me an arm and a leg.

2. Put the verb in the correct form (*needn't have / didn't need to*).

1. You (change) .... the oil. I had already taken the car to the shop.
2. My coffee was already sweetened, so I (put) .... any sugar in it. I drank it as it was.
3. You (bring) .... your portable. I could have lent you mine.
4. I (go) .... and fetch her. I sent the nurse instead.
5. You (bring) .... some champagne, but since you have, let's open it.
6. They (wait) .... too long. They were served very quickly.
7. The train was overdue. We (arrive) .... so early at the station.
8. I (take) .... a driving test. My American license was good as gold.
9. I used to live right in the centre of town. I (use) .... public transport to get to work.

3. Spot the possible mistakes and correct them. Write R for Right.

1. R / W............... They managed to fix the microwave oven. She needn't have to buy a new one.
2. R / W............... We need not take the car. The wedding was celebrated in the church next to our home.
3. R / W............... You didn't need write; you could've called.
4. R / W............... You needn't have came. The class was cancelled.
5. R / W............... I didn't need answer all the questions, but I did.

Correction

1. 1c - 2e - 3a - 4f - 5d - 6b

2. **1**. needn't have changed - **2**. didn't need to put - **3**. needn't have brought - **4**. didn't need to go - **5**. didn't need to bring - **6**. didn't need to wait - **7**. needn't have arrived - **8**. didn't need to take - **9**. didn't need to use

3. **1**. She didn't need to buy - **2**. We didn't need to take - **3**. You needn't have written - **4**. You needn't have come - **5**. I needn't have answered

52 WISH

1. Spot the possible mistakes and correct them. Write R for Right.

1. R / W............... I wish you don't have to leave today.
2. R / W............... I wish my car is fixed. I wouldn't have to walk.
3. R / W............... I wish he'd stop making so much noise when he eats.
4. R / W............... I wish she were talking so much nonsense.
5. R / W............... I wish he came with us. We wouldn't have got lost.
6. R / W............... I wish he could be operated on in Paris.
7. R / W............... Do you think the American colonies ever wish they have not gained their independence?
8. R / W............... She left but I wish she hadn't stayed a bit longer.

2. Write T (True) or F (False) for the statement that follows each numbered sentence.

1. I wish she were here with me! ⇨ She's far away : ......
2. I wish he'd stop grumbling! ⇨ He's getting on my nerves : ......
3. I wish it weren't so cold. ⇨ Temperatures are above zero : ......
4. What a pity he couldn't come! ⇨ I wish he came : ......
5. If only he hadn't been elected! ⇨ I regret his election : ......
6. I wish I had sold my house last year. ⇨ If only I hadn't sold it : ......

3. Rewrite the sentences using *wish*.

1. We regretted not having time to visit the Canyon de Chelly.
....
2. I would like my children to be less unruly.
....
3. I'm sorry I can't stop biting my nails.
....
4. I regret not being able to lend you any money right now.
....
5. I'm sorry I didn't see the ad in the local paper.
....
6. I regret bitterly ever having set eyes on you.
....
7. It's a pity they keep sending me all that junk mail!
....
8. I regret having bought that old jalopy. It keeps breaking down.
....

Correction

1. **1**. you didn't have - **2**. were fixed - **3**. R - **4**. she didn't talk - **5**. he'd come - **6**. R - **7**. they had not gained - **8**. she had stayed

2. 1T - 2T - 3F - 4F - 5T - 6F

3. **1**. We wished we had had time to visit the Canyon de Chelly. **2**. I wish my children weren't so unruly. **3**. I wish I could stop biting my nails. **4**. I wish I could lend you some money. **5**. I wish I had seen the ad in... . **6**. I really do wish I'd never set eyes on you. **7**. I wish they would stop sending me all that junk mail! **8**. I wish I hadn't bought that old jalopy.

53 SHOULD SUBJUNCTIVE (1)

1. Indicate whether *should* may be omitted (O) or not (NO) in the sentences.

1. Science (should) be taught by the process of discovery. ...... **2**. It is essential that you (should) be on time. ...... **3**. You (should) wear a tie to the ceremony. ...... **4**. It is normal that women (should) be paid the same as men for the same job. ...... **5**. It is incredible that he (should) have lost the final. ......

2. Rewrite the sentences using elements in brackets.

1. How disgraceful it is to see that some firms are making such huge profits whilst shedding jobs at the same time. ➪ (It is disgraceful that...)

....

2. I don't think it advisable for our company to take over our loss-making British competitor. ➪ (It is not advisable that...)

....

3. You'll find it essential to read all the books on the reading list before classes start in September. ➪ (It is essential that...)

....

4. He was ahead in the polls two weeks before the election. I find the fact that he lost incredible. ➪ (It is incredible that...)

....

3. Spot the possible mistakes and correct them. Write R for Right.

1. R / W............... It was horrible that the victims had their heads and hands cut off.
2. R / W............... It was pathetic that he is pleading with the teacher.
3. R / W............... It was sad that veterans should reduce to begging.
4. R / W............... It is strange that she should be in Paris.
5. R / W............... It is imperative that he posts the letter straight away.

4. Write sentences using the elements in brackets + *should*. Put the verb in the correct form.

1. (passport / it / necessary / you / have / your / renewed / is)

....

2. (term / find / long / be / only / sentenced / prison / right / I / normal / it / a)

....

3. (stricken / relief / it / urgent / area / to / send / the / is)

....

Correction

1. **1**. NO - **2**. O - **3**. NO - **4**. O - **5**. O

2. **1**. It is disgraceful that some firms should be making such huge profits whilst shedding jobs at the same time. **2**. It is not advisable that our company should take over... . **3**. It is essential that you should read all the books... . **4**. It is incredible that he should have lost.

3. **1**. should have had - **2**. should be pleading - **3**. should be reduced - **4**. R - **5**. he should post

4. **1**. It is necessary that you should have your passport renewed. **2**. I find it only right that he should have been sentenced to a long prison term. **3**. It's urgent that relief be sent to the stricken area.

54 SHOULD SUBJUNCTIVE (2)

1. Complete the sentences using the right noun.

disgrace - miracle - pity - reason - suggestions

1. It is a .... that he should have escaped unscathed.
2. It is a .... that former felons be denied the right to vote.
3. He's done a stellar job. There is no .... why he should resign.
4. Any .... that the government should have saved the bank were squelched by the Fed.
5. It's a .... turnout in US presidential elections should be so low.

2. Complete the sentences using the right verb in the correct tense.

advise - agree - demand - insist - recommend - suggest - urge

1. The board .... that production be outsourced in China.
2. The heads of state .... that an agreement on global warming be found as early as possible.
3. The European commissioners .... that negotiations should begin next year on the admission of Turkey.
4. The local authorities .... that the oil company be billed for the clean-up of the shores polluted by the oil spill.
5. The tobacco industry has .... to the illiberal idea that it should give up most forms of advertising,
6. Reacting to the school killing, the President .... that all gun sales be banned.
7. The tax authorities .... that the company submit all its tax records.

3. Match the numbered elements with the lettered ones and form a coherent sentence.

__1__. There's no reason - __2__. The state senate recommended - __3__. The judge ordered - __4__. It's disgraceful - __5__. It is an amazing feat - __6__. It's just my luck

a. .... that he should have had to beg for a leave of absence to go to his father's funeral.
b. .... that the car should break down in the middle of a storm.
c. .... why girls shouldn't be as good at math as boys are.
d. .... that the Americans should have sent a manned mission to Mars!
e. .... that marijuana should be made available for medical purposes.
f. .... that the company should be split into two.

Correction

1. **1**. miracle - **2**. disgrace - **3**. reason - **4**. suggestions - **5**. pity

2. **1**. suggested - **2**. recommended - **3**. advised - **4**. insisted - **5**. agreed - **6**. urged - **7**. demanded

3. 1c - 2e - 3f - 4a - 5d - 6b

55 SUBJUNCTIVE (REVIEW)

Circle the letter of the correct answer.

1. The EU demanded that the Russian troops ... from Ossetia at once.
a) withdraw b) might withdraw
c) are withdrawing d) did withdraw

2. The general asked that uniforms ... for the reception.
a) to be wore b) be worn c) are worn d) were worn

3. National security requires that partisan interests ... set aside for the present.
a) are b) be c) have d) were

4. That Mary ... dare speak in that tone of voice to me!
a) would b) will c) should d) shall

5. It was an odd thing that Jane ... for me so late.
a) will be waiting b) wait
c) were waiting d) should be waiting

6. Is it essential that petrol duties ... put up right now while most people are struggling to make both ends meet?
a) shouldn't be b) shouldn't c) may not be d) hadn't been

7. The police was urging everyone that there ... no violence.
a) might be b) should be c) were d) was

8. I would be most happy to provide any further information ... require it.
a) you would b) did you c) had you d) should you

9. A lot of people are saying he ... to resign from the government.
a) dares b) need c) should d) ought

10. Tell him I'll send a check tomorrow ... for immediate payment.
a) does he press b) did he press
c) would he press d) should he press

11. I woke up early so that I ... on time for my flight.
a) should be b) are c) will be d) have been

12. The imam insisted that the tourists ... the mosque during Ramadan.
a) should enter b) enter c) did not enter d) shouldn't enter

13. The coach insisted that Horatio ... fly half, even though he was much too slow for that position
a) plays b) play c) 'd play d) played

14. ... that as it may, the currency turmoil will have economic effects.
a) Should b) Be c) Would d) It is

15. Far ... from me to pry into someone else's problems. I'm not a cop!
a) it should b) it is c) be it d) it would

16. If their father came to pass away, ... the thought, I can't imagine what would happen to the six children.
a) perish b) perishes c) should perish d) perished

Correction

1a - 2b - 3b - 4c - 5d - 6a - 7b - 8d - 9d - 10d - 11a - 12d - 13b - 14b - 15c - 16a

56 ADVICE (SHOULD / OUGHT TO / HAD BETTER)

1. Spot the possible mistakes and correct them. Write R for Right.

1. R / W............... We'd better to stop now. I'm getting tired.

2. R / W............... I think that access to certain Internet sites ought be restricted.

3. R / W............... The Australians should win the Ashes. They had the better team.

4. R / W............... If you have time, you should have gone up crabbing to Maine, especially in autumn.

5. R / W............... He ought to have sold his Lehman stock. They're not likely to go up in the near future.

2. Combine the numbered elements with the lettered ones.

1. They're looking for a cashier. **2.** You'd better leave now, **3.** He's going on a safari in Tanzania. **4.** The planet's oil resources are being depleted. **5.** He's pushing himself too hard. If he doesn't watch it he will have a heart attack. **6.** The radio said a tornado was coming our way. **7.** Running for president is no easy task.	**a.** or you're going to be late. **b.** We'd better start conserving energy. **c.** You'd better board up the windows. **d.** He should take a few days off. **e.** you'd better have an army of volunteers, loads of cash and plenty of guts. **f.** Should I apply for the job? **g.** He should get inoculated against yellow fever.

3. Complete the sentences using the verbs from the list in the correct form.

ask / break down / consult / drink / get / smoke / wait / wear

1. He can't lift those heavy boxes with his bad back. He'd better .... his brother to do it. **2**. "Captain, one of the tanker's engines ...." "Then I think we should call out a tug." **3**. "Shall we leave now?" "If I were you I should .... until the rain lets up." **4**. "You'd better not .... before the journey or you won't be able to drive." **5**. You know how complicated doing one's tax returns is! You'd better .... an accountant to do it for you. **6**. The party leader should .... with the rank and file before making hasty decisions. **7**. I'd rather you didn't .... in front of the kids. **8**. Even on Fridays, the boss would rather the employees didn't .... jeans.

Correction

1. **1**. We'd better stop - **2**. ought to be - **3**. they have the better team *or* should have won - **4**. you should go - **5**. He ought to sell

2. 1f - 2a - 3g - 4b - 5d - 6c - 7e

3. **1**. get - **2**. has broken down - **3**. wait - **4**. drink - **5**. ask - **6**. should have consulted / should consult - **7**. smoke - **8**. wear

57 DEDUCTION (MAY / MIGHT / COULD / MUST / HAVE TO / CAN'T)

1. Match each fact with the correct deduction.

1. He can't speak. **2.** He can't have robbed the bank. **3.** Sally doesn't answer the phone. **4.** Bee colonies are disappearing rapidly. **5.** Someone's knocking on the door. **6.** Is he still working with Morgan's? **7.** Could you have met his brother? **8.** She came home late but had no key. **9.** Her eyes are red. **10.** The cat's gone.	**a.** Who could that be? **b.** So she may not have been able to get in. **c.** He was in jail at that time. **d.** Don't panic. It can't be far. **e.** She might be in the garden cutting the grass. **f.** Very likely. We were neighbors 15 years ago. **g.** He's a mute. **h.** It may be due to overuse of pesticides. **i.** I'm not sure. He might not be. **j.** She must have been crying.

2. Give a negative meaning to the following sentences.

1. He must have stolen the money. ....

2. He may have committed the crime. ....

3. You could have guessed it was poetry. ....

4. He must be in love. ....

3. Circle the correct answer.

1. Harry didn't wave to me so he must have known / can't have known I was there. **2**. Look the shop's closed. It can have gone / may have gone out of business. **3**. "Wasn't that Jennifer in the blue convertible?" "It could / couldn't. She's moved to Australia." **4**. The Angkor Vat temple was built in the early 12th century. This can have been / must have been a great civilization. **5**. Look! The window's open. Someone can't have broken / may have broken into the house. **6**. "Could John have been at home last night?" "He had to have been / could have been." **7**. He's only 23. He may be / can't be a doctor. **8**. He can't have lost / may have lost so much weight so quickly! He can be / must be ill.

Correction

1. 1g - 2c - 3e - 4h - 5a - 6i - 7f - 8b - 9j - 10d

2. **1**. He can't have stolen the money. **2**. He can't have committed the crime. **3**. You couldn't have guessed it was poetry. **4**. He can't be in love.

3. **1**. can't have known - **2**. may have gone - **3**. couldn't - **4**. must have been - **5**. may have broken - **6**. could have been - **7**. can't be - **8**. can't have / must be

58 NECESSITY / NON NECESSITY

1. Match each result with its direct cause.

Cause	Result
1. Mother has been taken to hospital. **2.** I have to wear glasses all the time **3.** She has had to wear braces **4.** You must take an eye test **5.** We must not shrink from confrontation **6.** Liz, you must stop seeing Luke. **7.** Even a journey of a thousand miles **8.** Sorry for being late but	**a.** He's no good for you. **b.** I had to wait ages for a bus. **c.** if you want to get your driving license. **d.** should I want to preserve my eyes. **e.** must begin with a single step. **f.** I must go and see her. **g.** since she was five years old. **h.** if vital American interests are challenged.

2. Express the following ideas in the past tense.

1. You must all stop what you're doing and listen carefully.

....

2. She mustn't be left home alone.

....

3. He doesn't have to read the whole book.

....

4. If you want to succeed, you must work as hard as you can.

....

5. We have to do it all over again.

....

6. He says the Democratic candidate is not to be trusted.

....

7. You are to take one pill every other day for two weeks.

....

8. You have to lay the table for twelve.

....

3. Put the verbs in the correct form (*didn't need to / needn't have*).

1. We (read) .... all of *King Lear* for the first class, but we had to have read at least the first act. **2**. I (wake) .... him up, for he was already fully dressed when I knocked on his bedroom door. **3**. We (wait) .... long. He was back in a jiffy.

Correction

1. 1f - 2d - 3g - 4c - 5h - 6a - 7e - 8b

2. **1**. We all had to stop / were doing - **2**. She was not to be left home alone - **3**. He didn't have to read - **4**. if you wanted / you had to / you could - **5**. We had to - **6**. He said the Democratic candidate was not to be trusted - **7**. You had to take / You were to take - **8**. You had to lay

3. **1**. We didn't need to read - **2**. I didn't need to wake him up - **3**. We didn't need to wait.

59 PROBABILITY

1. Rank the sentences according to three degrees of probability : S (= sure or quasi sure), P (= possibility), U (= lesser possibility).

1. "Will you marry me?" he asked. "Yes, I *will*", she answered. ....
2. I may come after all. ....
3. We might have a little bit of snow by the end of the day. ....
4. You must be Bill's brother! ....
5. There is no answer. They must have left. ....
6. He may have been prevented from leaving the country. ....
7. He might have decided to stay overnight. ....
8. You might have left your glasses in the classroom. ....
9. "You will come to dinner, won't you?" "Of course, I will." ....
10. It might rain this afternoon. ....

2. Rewrite the sentences using modals expressing probability.

1. Perhaps she's got a cold.
....
2. There is no doubt in my mind that he's guilty as hell.
....
3. "US president to stop over in Georgia" (newspaper headlines)
....
4. It's highly likely that the child ran away from home.
....
5. The chances are that her home was broken into to steal her manuscript.
....
6. I'm positive that's the very man I saw with the little girl.
....
7. Perhaps the flight was delayed.
....
8. Perhaps Arsenal won't win the championship after all.
....
9. Where's Pete? I'm sure he's in his room, working.
....

3. Rewrite sentences using the appropriate modal.

1. Are you sure she's left? That's impossible. ➪ She ....
2. I'm positive this church was built in the 12th century. ➪ It ....
3. Perhaps the hotel never received confirmation of the booking. ➪ The hotel ....

Correction

1. 1S - 2P - 3U - 4S - 5S - 6P - 7U - 8U - 9S - 10U

2. **1**. She may have a cold. **2**. He must be guilty. **3**. The US President will be stopping over in Georgia. **4**. The child must have run away from home. **5**. Her home may well have been broken into... . **6**. That must be the very man... **7**. The flight may have been delayed. **8**. Arsenal may not win the championship. **9**. He must be in his room... .

3. 1. She can't have left. **2**. It must have been built... **3**. The hotel may never have received

60 PREFERENCE (PREFER / WOULD PREFER / WOULD RATHER)

1. Spot the possible mistakes and correct them. Write R for Right.

1. R / W............... I'd rather to play video games than go out with the snotty kids next door.
2. R / W............... I'd rather live in Manhattan to the Bronx any day.
3. R / W............... Do you prefer stay in or go out tonight?
4. R / W............... I'd prefer to have Italian food for lunch.
5. R / W............... I'd rather you stay home tonight. You've been out three times this week already.
6. R / W............... Sarah prefers play the piano whenever she has some free time.
7. R / W............... Sam prefers action movies than comedies.
8. R / W............... My daughter prefers hiking than swimming.
9. R / W............... Would you rather he not come with us?
10. R / W............... I'd rather send an e-mail than write a letter.
11. R / W............... I wouldn't rather have dessert. I'm on a diet.
12. R / W............... "Would you like some raspberries?" "I'd rather no. I'm allergic to them."

2. Express preferences with *would prefer / would rather + to / than.*

1. go to the movies / watch films on television ....
2. study math / study languages ....
3. have tea / coffee ....
4. be sunning on a beach / sit at my office ....

3. Put the verbs in brackets in the correct tense.

1. I'd rather you (leave) .... now instead of spending the night here.
2. I'd rather you (take) .... the dog with you than leave her in the kennel to bark all night.
3. I'd rather (kick) .... a football around than (sit) .... in class daydreaming.
4. She's pregnant. She'd rather (not drive) .... too much.
5. I'd rather you (not stray) .... too far. I don't want you to get lost.
6. Most patients would rather (tell) .... the truth than (lie) .... to.
7. I'd rather you (talk) .... it over to me instead of making that rash decision by yourself. Unfortunately, it's too late now.

Correction

1. **1**. I'd rather play - **2**. I'd rather live in Manhattan than the Bronx - **3**. staying / going - **4**. R - **5**. I'd rather you stayed - **6**. Sarah prefers to play the piano - **7**. prefers action movies to comedies - **8**. hiking to swimming - **9**. Would you rather he didn't come - **10**. R - **11**. I'd rather not have - **12**. I'd rather not

2. **1**. I'd rather go to the movies than watch films on television. **2**. I'd rather study math than study languages. **3**. I'd rather have tea than coffee. **4**. I'd rather be sunning... than sitting at my office.

3. **1**. left - **2**. took - **3**. kick / sit - **4**. not drive - **5**. you didn't stray - **6**. be told the truth / be lied - **7**. had talked

61 REQUEST

1. Complete the sentences using expressions from the list.

buy some coffee - call back later - mind driving - hold the line - lend me some money - turn the heat up

1. Can you .... , please? I'll see what I can do.
2. Could you .... ? I'm broke.
3. Would you mind if I .... It's freezing in here.
4. Will you .... on the way home ? There's none left.
5. I'm afraid he's busy right now. Could you .... ?
6. Do you .... ? I can't see very well at night.

2. Circle the letter(s) of the correct answer(s).

1. Jenna, would you show me how to use the fax machine?
a) Yes, sure b) Yes, I would
2. Would you mind if I borrowed the car for today? Mine is in the shop.
a) Not at all b) Yes
3. Will you go to the PTA meeting at 5 P.M.?
a) No, I won't b) Sorry, I have a meeting at 6.
4. Can you tell the professor I'll be late for class today?
a) Yes, I will b) Yes, I will be able to
5. I'm cold. Would you shut the window, please?
a) Certainly b) Yes, I would
6. Professor Jones, may I talk to you for a minute?
a) Sure, James! b) You may, James
7. I think I need two more weeks to finish my paper, if that's okay with you.
a) That is b) I don't see why not
8. Excuse me, do you know where Route 66 starts?
a) I'm sorry I do b) I'm sorry I don't
9. Excuse me, I'm looking for the History department. Is it it?
a) Yes, it is it b) Yes, you're in the right place
10. Would you mind waiting for a few minutes?
a) I would b) Not at all
11. Would you mind giving me a hand with my luggage?
a) No, I would b) Not at all
12. Could you keep an eye on my satchel?
a) Sure b) By all means
13. Will applications still be accepted after Friday?
a) No, they won't b) Yes, they will
14. Let's go to the beach ...?
a) will we b) shall we

Correction

1. **1**. hold the line - **2**. lend me some money - **3**. turn the heat up - **4**. buy some coffee - **5**. call back later - **6**. mind driving

2. 1a - 2a - 3b - 4a - 5a - 6a - 7b - 8b - 9b - 10b - 11b - 12a - 13a/b - 14b

62 REGRET

1. Rewrite the sentences using the modal in brackets to express regret.

1. I didn't invite Megan to the party. Now she's angry with me.
(ought to) ....

2. It's a pity I didn't bring my camcorder for John's wedding.
(wish) ....

3. I lost my parking ticket. The attendant charged me $24 for just an hour.
(should) ....

4. I ate too much chocolate. I feel sick.
(should) ....

5. Primo Levi committed suicide because of his experience in Auschwitz, but we just don't know.
(might) ....

6. I didn't have enough money to tip the waiter. Why didn't Jenna lend me some?
(could) ....

7. Damn! I wanted seats but the concert is sold out.
(wish) ....

2. Write T (True) or F (False) for the statement that follows each numbered sentence.

1. I wish I could buy that car. ⇨ I bought the car : ......
2. What a pity Thomas couldn't come! ⇨ Thomas came : ......
3. I wish I had known the answers before the test. ⇨ I probably failed : ......
4. She's a beautiful young woman. I wish I were 30 years younger!
⇨ I'm barely 40 : ......
5. I wish Lauren would follow my advice from time to time.
⇨ Lauren is pig-headed : ......

3. Put the verbs in brackets in the correct form.

1. "Did you enjoy the novel I lent you last week?" "No, it was awful. I wish I (not waste) .... my time reading it." **2**. Don't you wish you (come) .... earlier? **3**. I keep getting those cranky calls. I wish I (go) .... ex-directory. **4**. Charles Laughton often wished he (can / direct) .... more than just one movie. **5**. The day will come when you will wish you (heed) .... my advice. **6**. Don't most Americans wish they (can / make) .... more money?

Correction

1. **1**. I ought to have invited her - **2**. I wish I had brought my camcorder - **3**. He shouldn't have charged - **4**. I shouldn't have eaten - **5**. He might have committed - **6**. She could have lent me - **7**. I wish I had thought about booking earlier.

2. 1F - 2F - 3T - 4F - 5T

3. **1**. hadn't wasted - **2**. had come - **3**. had gone - **4**. had been able to direct - **5**. had heeded - **6**. could make

63 REGRET ABOUT THE PAST

1. Combine the numbered elements with the lettered ones.

1. These pears are rotten. **2.** It was almost midnight now. **3.** I ought to have taken that job. **4.** He wished he had gone to college. **5.** What with all the work you did! **6.** He failed to hand in his paper in time. **7.** How much did you say you spent? **8.** Everyone wishes the coup had been successful, **9.** She wished she had not missed the football game,	**a.** Today, the only jobs he can get are low-paid. **b.** then the dictator would have been toppled. **c.** She ought to have come home at least two hours ago. **d.** although there's not much she might have done to prevent her son's concussion. **e.** That was a big mistake to turn it down. **f.** You should have been more careful with *my* money. **g.** You shouldn't have bought them. **h.** You should not have flunked the exam. **i.** He ought to have told the lecturer.

2. Write T (True) or F (False) for the statement that follows each numbered sentence.

1. You should not have called the teacher home.
He didn't call the teacher : ......

2. She ought to have been warned about the dangers of swimming off shore.
I'm sorry I didn't tell her : ......

3. Chloe would have made a brilliant physician.
She works as a cashier : ......

4. I'm soaked through.
I wish I had brought my umbrella : ......

5. Much of the 2008 financial crisis on Wall Street could have been prevented through legislation.
All hell broke loose : ......

6. She wishes she had not had an abortion.
She didn't keep the baby : ......

Correction

1. 1g - 2c - 3e - 4a - 5h - 6i - 7f - 8b - 9d

2. 1F - 2T - 3T - 4T - 5T - 6T

64 MODALS (REVIEW) (1)

Circle the letter of the correct answer.

1. You ... do that to your kid sister!
a) would better b) must not to c) oughtn't d) mustn't

2. Few people ... imagined at the time that he was to be elected.
a) will have b) could have c) would had d) were to have

3. There's no ice in the fridge. There ... a power failure.
a) must have been b) was to be
c) might d) should be

4. I can't find my wallet. Someone ... my pocket while I was on the bus.
a) might pick b) must have picked
c) has been picking d) had picked

5. According to the regulations, all goods entering the country ... pay duties.
a) had to b) ought to c) should d) were bound to

6. You ... sent a letter to your aunt when you were in Idaho.
a) should b) will c) must d) ought to have

7. I'm not sure where Angela is. I think she ... to a party tonight.
a) must have gone b) might have gone
c) had to go d) any of these answers

8. Keep today's paper that I ... it later.
a) am to read b) should read c) shall read d) might read

9. You ... us a visit to see our new Rauschenberg painting.
a) should pay b) would pay c) should pay to d) would pay to

10. He ... to fix the computer when it broke down. It works fine now.
a) was able to b) could c) could have d) can

11. Passengers ... that the bus service had been cancelled.
a) ought to be informed b) should inform
c) ought to have been informed d) should have informed

12. "I'm sure any twit ... climb Ben Nevis if they tried."
a) will be able to b) was able to c) can d) could

13. She fell sick and ... to see a doctor.
a) must b) has to c) had to d) must to

14. There's plenty of beer left. You ... go shopping.
a) don't need b) needn't to c) don't have d) needn't

15. I'm on my way. I ... be there in ten minutes.
a) should b) ought c) must d) am able

16. Yesterday was Columbus Day. I ... go to work.
a) had not to b) didn't had to c) didn't have to d) needn't

17. She tried to contact you, but your phone ... busy. She never got to you.
a) must've been b) should've been c) ought to be d) may be

Correction

1d ; order or interdiction from the speaker - **2b** - **3a** ; deduction - **4b** ; deduction - **5b** ; ought to = rules - **6d** ; past - **7d** ; must have gone = deduction, might have gone = possibility ; had to go = obligation - **8d** - **9a** ; advice - **10a** ; was able to = action which has been validated - **11c** - **12d** - **13c** - **14d** - **15a** - **16c** ; non necessity - **17a** ; deduction

65 MODALS (REVIEW) (2)

1. Spot the possible mistakes in the underlined modals and correct them. Write R for Right.

1. R / W............... Jack's flight from Australia took more than 15 hours. He can be exhausted after such a long flight.

2. R / W............... If you want to get a better feeling for how the city is laid out, you may walk downtown and explore its streets.

3. R / W............... Climbing to the top of a mountain can be hazardous if you're not well-prepared.

4. R / W............... You must to fasten your seat belt when you drive or you couldn't drive.

5. R / W............... The man you saw at St Andrews ought not to be Professor Wisdom—he's on sabbatical at the moment.

6. R / W............... He mustn't be far away, he said he'd only be a minute.

7. R / W............... Joshua, may you hold your breath for a minute?

8. R / W............... Have you seen her engagement ring? It can cost Tim an arm and a leg.

9. R / W............... Might you look after my plants while I'm gone? If they don't get enough water, they shall be able to die.

10. R / W............... You have not to take your umbrella today. The weatherman said it was going to be a fine day.

2. Complete the sentences using the right modal.

1. When you have teenagers in the house, you (watch) .... it when they surf on the Internet. **2**. Look! Laura's glasses are on the table. She (leave) .... them last night. **3**. Garth, you (chew) .... with your mouth open like a sick whale? Geez, it's making me sick watching you eat those broccolis. **4**. "I don't know why she's crying." "It (be) .... what you said about her hairstyle. She's very touchy on that subject." **5**. "I guess I (attend) .... this meeting," said Samuel. "You (take) .... a cab if you want to be on time," said Jennifer. **6**. "Who (send) .... those flowers?" "It (be) .... Jessica, to thank you for the job." **7**. Megan's been awarded a fellowship from Berkeley. It will cover her tuition fees. She no longer (worry) .... about the cost of her education. **8**. "Oh my God, Sam's been knocked unconscious." "Don't move him. He (suffer) .... a concussion. Call an ambulance." **9**. If he won the jackpot, he actually (leave) .... his job and travel across the wide world. **10**. (At the restaurant) You (try) .... our Crock of Oyster Stew or perhaps the Cape Cod Cherrystones. They're both delicious. **11**. You (check) .... the air pressure in your tires. We wouldn't have got a flat tire.

Correction

1. **1**. must - **2**. should - **3**. R - **4**. must fasten / can't drive - **5**. can't have been - **6**. can't - **7**. can - **8**. must have cost - **9**. Could / they may *or* might die - **10**. don't need to / need not take / don't have to

2. **1**. should (advice) - **2**. must have left (probability) - **3**. do you have to chew (habit) - **4**. must have been (deduction) - **5**. have to attend / 'd better attend (advice) / ought to take (suggestion) - **6**. could have sent (possibility) / must have been (deduction / probability) - **7**. needs to worry / has to worry (non-necessity) - **8**. may have suffered (possibility) - **9**. might actually leave - **10**. might (invitation) - **11**. ought to have checked (reproach)

66 PASSIVE (1)

1. Say whether the following sentences are active (A) or passive (P).

1. .... The Battle of Gettysburg was fought in Pennsylvania.
2. .... The result arrived at was not deemed satisfactory by the chairman.
3. .... The book sold millions.
4. .... Your essay reads extremely well despite the ghastly spelling.
5. .... Your paper must be handed in by next Thursday.
6. .... He's been found at last.
7. .... He's never had his license endorsed.
8. .... She's used the video recorder for the first time.

2. Put the sentences into the passive.

1. (When / America / discover?)
....
2. (When / the next EU summit / hold?)
....
3. (What / coca / use for / in the Middle Ages?)
....
4. (When / the Wild West / conquer?)
....
5. (It / try / can / not / make / work) (*2 passives*)
....

3. Put the sentences into the passive.

1. The bill (debate) .... by MPs this morning. **2**. The government unexpectedly (defeat) .... last night in a backbench revolt. **3**. The guerrillas soon (drive) .... back by the armed forces. **4**. He (tell) .... by the airline that his luggage would be forwarded to his home as soon as possible and his next trip upgraded to first class. **5**. After reading the article in *The Sun*, the prime minister (see) .... by everybody present to be very angry. **6**. Because of a storm warning, the launch (postpone) .... again. **7**. More than 4m square feet of new business space (build) .... in Los Angeles county over the past few years. **8**. The teenagers (allege) .... to have set fire to the school because they were resentful of their teachers. **9**. All that (could / see) .... of the remnants of the gutted building was the charred debris of the castle's past grandeur. **10**. Any newly elected government (can / expect / give) .... the benefit of the doubt by the public. **11**. The landlord didn't know how the fire had started, all he could say was that it (might / cause) .... by a faulty boiler.

Correction

1. 1P - 2P - 3A - 4A - 5P - 6P - 7A - 8A

2. **1**. When was America discovered? **2**. When will the next EU summit be held? **3**. What was coca used for in the Middle Ages? **4**. When was the Wild West conquered? **5**. It's been tried but could not be made to work.

3. **1**. is being debated - **2**. was unexpectedly defeated - **3**. were soon driven back / will be soon driven back - **4**. was told - **5**. was seen - **6**. has been postponed again - **7**. have been built - **8**. are alleged - **9**. could be seen - **10**. can expect to be given - **11**. might have been caused

67 PASSIVE (2)

1. Put the sentences into the passive using a person as subject.

1. Someone told the students who had arrived late to wait outside.

....

2. They helped the freshmen to register for the fall term.

....

3. They asked the photographer to take lots of pictures of the bride and bridegroom.

....

4. They will take good care of his grandmother in the nursing home.

....

5. After the ceremony they treated us to a concert of classical music.

....

2. Put the sentences into the passive voice.

1. The engineers looked into the problem.

....

2. They eventually arrived at the expected result.

....

3. They frown on smoking in America.

....

4. The customs authorities turned the journalist back and escorted him straight to his plane. (*2 passives*)

....

5. The management took him to court when they found out he had embezzled thousands of dollars from the firm.

....

3. Put the verbs in italics into the passive when possible.

The candidate said that he would not *re-nationalize* all privatized companies and would *take* a pragmatic approach to state-controlled companies which do not *provide* a public service. He said that he would *limit* welfare spending, *free* prices and capital movement and *drop* the idea of a promised cut in the working week. He would *stabilize* the overall tax burden and would then *reduce* it. Although he did not specifically *mention* public spending in the party's manifesto, he said that he *would seek* to *reduce* the public deficit.

....

....

....

....

Correction

1. **1**. The students who had arrived late were told to wait outside. **2**. The freshmen were helped to register for the fall term. **3**. The photographer was asked to take lots of pictures of the bride and bridegroom. **4**. Good care of his grandmother will be taken in the nursing home. **5**. After the ceremony we were treated to a concert of classical music.

2. **1**. The problem was looked into by the engineers. **2**. The expected result was eventually arrived at. **3**. Smoking is frowned on in America. **4**. The journalist was turned back and escorted straight to his plane. **5**. He was taken to court...

3. The candidate said that all privatized companies would not **be re-nationalized** and a pragmatic approach to state-controlled companies which do not *provide* a public service **would be taken**. He said that welfare spending **would be limited**, prices and capital movement **would be freed** and the idea of a promised cut in the working week **dropped**. The overall tax burden **would be stabilized** and then **reduced**. Although public spending in the party's manifesto **was not specifically mentioned**, he said that he *would seek* to *reduce* the public deficit / a reduction in the public deficit **would be sought**.

68 TRANSITIVE / INTRANSITIVE VERBS

1. Spot the possible mistakes and correct them. Write R for Right.

1. R / W............... Those who disobey to my orders will be punished.
2. R / W............... He taught to the little girl how to read and write.
3. R / W............... He stressed on the last two syllables of the word.
4. R / W............... I envy to him his extraordinary command of languages.
5. R / W............... He had forgotten his keys and couldn't enter his flat.
6. R / W............... The accused answered to the judge's questions truthfully.
7. R / W............... His parents promised to him a new computer for Easter.
8. R / W............... He borrowed $1,000 to his father.

2. Insert the right preposition.

1. Several MPs were at the state dinner ...... which the US President attended at Buckingham Palace. **2**. Politicians always try to please ...... all men. **3**. When the principal enters ...... the classroom, the children stand up. **4**. The bank manager couldn't account ...... the disappearance of several thousand euros. **5**. Someone has just handed ...... Professor Watson a message. **6**. As Gerry was sick, she couldn't attend ...... the meeting. **7**. Nobody could have survived ...... such a fall. **8**. Globalization will probably benefit ...... the interests of emerging countries. **9**. She married ...... a wealthy old New England family. **10**. He stole the company's secrets and sold them ...... the competitors.

3. Circle the letter of the correct answer.

1. He bought his car ... a crooked Ford dealer.
a) at b) from c) in d) of
2. Those who are caught stealing ... the store will be prosecuted.
a) at b) of c) ø d) from
3. I explained the principle of the electoral college ... the students.
a) at b) from c) to d) at
4. Why don't you tell me ... it?
a) of b) about c) ø d) from
5. The foreign secretary asked the ambassador ... his immediate resignation.
a) for b) ø c) of d) about
6. Please refrain ... in the library as other people are trying to work.
a) to talk b) talking c) from talking d) talk
7. Who did you borrow it ...?
a) from b) at c) by d) to

Correction

1. **1**. disobey my order - **2**. taught the little girl - **3**. stressed the last two syllables - **4**. I envy him - **5**. R - **6**. answered the judge - **7**. promised him - **8**. He borrowed... from his father

2. **1**. ø - **2**. ø - **3**. ø - **4**. for - **5**. ø - **6**. ø - **7**. ø - **8**. ø - **9**. into - **10**. to

3. 1b - 2d - 3c - 4b - 5a - 6c - 7a

69 VERBS + PREPOSITION (1)

1. Spot the possible mistakes and correct them. Write R for Right.

1. R / W.............. The heads of state are discussing about the future of the planet.
2. R / W.............. Today, many parents fear of their children's safety if they play out in the street.
3. R / W.............. The witness has been accused with lying to the grand jury
4. R / W.............. The law should prevent from temporary cash-flow difficulties by forcing solvent debtors to settle their bills.
5. R / W.............. Their original offer provided delayed repayment of the loan if borrowers came up against unexpected problems.
6. R / W.............. Faced with the horrifying drugs numbers, America's officials sometimes yearn after tighter borders.
7. R / W.............. The banks had been warned several times of the danger of investing too heavily on the American markets.
8. R / W.............. I offered to pay the bill but she wouldn't hear from it.
9. R / W.............. When Microsoft offered him a job, he leapt after it.
10. R / W.............. Following the restructuring of the German company, thousands of employees will be transferred in India.

2. Complete the sentences using the right preposition.

1. The new law against juvenile offenders threatens to deprive many households .... their family allowances. **2**. Like most new technologies, e-mail has its limitations. It can never substitute .... face-to-face conversation. **3**. He is suspected .... having masterminded the 1963 Great Train Robbery. **4**. She's fed up with London. She's thinking .... moving back to the country. **5**. The customer had forgotten his wallet so I sent one of the clerks .... him. **6**. Although profits are down this quarter, the company is hoping .... better results over the next six months. **7**. Relief agencies appealed .... emergency aid for Haiti, which is enduring its worst floods in 40 years. **8**. The UN warned Russia .... the dangers of not complying ...... the Security Council's resolution. **9**. They wouldn't be pushed into making a decision and said they would need some time to think it .... **10**. I eventually heard .... him after three months' silence. **11**. She smiled .... me as I walked past her and so I winked .... her. **12**. They hired a child-carer to attend .... the baby while they were at work. **13**. The price of crude oil has risen .... its highest level since the 1973 oil crisis. It now stands .... $156 a barrel.

Correction

1. **1**. discuss + ø - **2**. fear for - **3**. accused of - **4**. prevent + ø - **5**. provided for - **6**. yearn for - **7**. warned about - **8**. hear of - **9**. leapt at - **10**. transferred to

2. **1**. of - **2**. for - **3**. of - **4**. about / of - **5**. after - **6**. for - **7**. for - **8**. about / with - **9**. over - **10**. from - **11**. at / at - **12**. to - **13**. to / at

70 VERBS + PREPOSITION (2)

1. Rewrite the sentences using verbs in brackets. Add the right preposition.

1. Responsibility for the crane accident was the operator's. (BLAME) ....

2. He knows how to protect his own interests. (LOOK) ....

3. The year he spent studying English abroad really helped him improve his self confidence. (BENEFIT) ....

4. You couldn't see the house from the road because of the wood. (CONCEAL) ....

5. Small-time city-centre stores cannot compete with the big shopping centers in either price or personal service. (RIVAL) ....

6. Somebody got into her flat and stole her plasma screen. (BREAK) ....

2. Circle the letter of the correct answer.

1. The FBI arrested a man suspected ... war crimes.
a) with b) of c) from d) to

2. Do you know Michael?" "I know ... him, but I've never met him."
a) of b) about c) from d) ø

3. She doesn't make enough money. She's thinking ... moving to the US.
a) of b) about c) to d) ø

4. The photographer asked the newly-weds to smile ... the camera.
a) before b) ø c) to d) at

5. Explain ... us why you are so late.
a) ø b) for c) to d) at

6. If the sea encroaches any further ... the sand dunes, the beach cottages on top are likely to be washed away.
a) against b) on c) at d) over

7. The US entered ... a free-trade agreement with Mexico and Canada a few years ago.
a) into b) in c) ø d) under

8. Salzburg has banned cars ... its center, turning it over ... pedestrians.
a) into / to b) of / with c) ø / after d) from / to

9. I blamed ... leaving my umbrella behind.
a) me for b) me to c) myself of d) myself for

10. The customer complained ... the manager ... the food.
a) to / of b) with / from c) to / about d) at / to

11. Business thrives ... challenges, novelty and experience.
a) by b) on c) in d) with

Correction

1. **1**. The operator was **blamed for** the crane accident. **2**. He knows how to **look after** himself. **3**. He **benefited from** his year abroad studying English. **4**. The house was **concealed from** the road by the wood. **5**. Small-time city-centre stores cannot **compete with** the big shopping centers in either price or personal service. **6**. Her flat was **broken into**.

2. 1b - 2a - 3a - 4d - 5c - 6b - 7a - 8d - 9d - 10c - 11b

71 MAKE / DO

1. *Make* or *do*? Circle the odd man out.

	a	*b*	*c*	*d*
1.	research	a suggestion	a decision	a point
2.	noise	a speech	trouble	a problem
3.	a cup of tea	nothing	the shopping	homework
4.	a difference	damage	progress	a gesture
5.	a favor	peace	an impression	allowances

2. Spot the possible mistakes and correct them. Write R for Right.

1. R / W............... If you want to make well in business, you'll have to do more of an effort.

2. R / W............... We'll have to make without a holiday this year as money is so tight

3. R / W............... You have done a serious mistake in doing business with such people.

4. R / W............... Thousands of workers have been done redundant at Ford over the past few years.

5. R / W............... So far no real damage has been made.

6. R / W............... They feel they have done the right choice.

3. Insert *make* or *do* in the correct tense.

1. Considerable headway .... in the peace talks so far. **2**. Forty years in therapy .... him no good at all. He is a ruthless, self-centered hypochondriac. **3**. Enormous progress .... in the last 25 years towards understanding how cells become malignant. **4**. He claimed that the real reason for his imprisonment was that he .... himself a nuisance by demanding rights for his minority. **5**. New management methods could .... wonders. And believe me, it .... sense too. **6**. On the whole, America .... a better job than any other country of balancing personal freedom against the general interest. **7**. "Jurassic Park" .... box-office history chiefly because of the way lifelike dinosaurs chased people and occasionally caught them.

4. Insert the right preposition.

1. There is a lot of money to be made .... property transactions in New York. **2**. The mugger threatened to do me .... if I didn't hand over my wallet, which I did. **3**. The athletes will do their hair .... in a bun to keep it out of their eyes. **4**. This weekend we plan to make .... St Moritz.

Correction

1. **1a** ; do research - **2d** ; do a problem - **3a** ; make a cup of tea - **4b** ; do damage - **5a** ; do (sb) a favor

2. **1**. do well in business / make more of an effort - **2**. do without - **3**. have made a serious mistake / R - **4**. have been made redundant - **5**. has been done - **6**. have made the right choice

3. **1**. has been made - **2**. did - **3**. has been made - **4**. made - **5**. do / would make - **6**. does - **7**. made

4. **1**. on / out of - **2**. over - **3**. up - **4**. for

72 COUNTABLE / UNCOUNTABLE NOUNS

1. Spot the possible mistakes and correct them. Write R for Right.

1. R / W.............. He's made many progress since last year.
2. R / W.............. I've told you much time before.
3. R / W.............. He's lazy. He doesn't like a work.
4. R / W.............. All the evidences suggest that a fifth industrial revolution is well under way.
5. R / W.............. The barracks was closed after the troops pulled out.
6. R / W.............. Economics were at the heart of the last campaign.
7. R / W.............. How many luggage will you have? Only a few.
8. R / W.............. He's been doing researches on stem cells.
9. R / W.............. She's made cake for the party tomorrow.
10. R / W.............. Information zip from one country to another at the click of a mouse.
11. R / W.............. Your luggage is far too heavy. Let me carry them.
12. R / W.............. Between their diverging views, there's room for negotiation.

2. Insert the correct article (*a* / *an* / *ø*).

1. He gave us ...... advice on what to take with us. **2**. I'm sorry I can't come. I have ...... homework to do. **3**. She's doing ...... research into ...... English teenage slang for her university project. **4**. You'll need ...... rice if you want to make a Chinese meal. **5**. Judith's getting ...... divorce? That's ...... interesting news. **6**. I have to buy ...... film for the holiday. I think I'll get about five rolls. **7**. We had ...... beautiful weather and ...... food in Tuscany. **8**. Contrary to ...... popular belief, ... part-time employment is not on the rise in America.

3. Circle the correct answer (quantifiers).

1. I'd like a little / little milk with my coffee. **2**. He makes many / much money. **3**. He hasn't made many / much progress since I last saw him. **4**. He has very little / few hair left on his head. **5**. How much / many people attended the conference? **6**. They ran into a little / a few trouble with the police. **7**. They received a little / a few news last night. **8**. I have few / little information on the earthquake. **9**. I'm surprised she spends so many / much, because I know how few / little she earns. **10**. They had a few / little idea of how to assess the project's feasibility. **11**. Several / Much works by Klein are on exhibition at the MOMA. **12**. We can't hire her. She doesn't have many / much experience.

Correction

1. **1**. much progress - **2**. many times - **3**. ø work - **4**. evidence suggests - **5**. R - **6**. was - **7**. much / a little - **8**. research - **9**. a cake - **10**. zips - **11**. it - **12**. R

2. **1**. ø - **2**. ø - **3**. ø / ø - **4**. ø - **5**. a / ø - **6**. ø - **7**. ø / ø - **8**. ø / ø

3. **1**. a little - **2**. much - **3**. much - **4**. little - **5**. many - **6**. a little - **7**. a little - **8**. little - **9**. much / little - **10**. little - **11**. Several - **12**. much

73 PROPER NOUNS

1. Spot the possible mistakes and correct them. Write R for Right.

1. R / W............... The *Titanic* struck an iceberg while crossing Atlantic.
2. R / W............... The Mediterranean is one of the most crowded spots in the summer time.
3. R / W............... Barbados is a small island in West Indies.
4. R / W............... The Watergate is an impressive building rising next to Potomac in Washington, D.C.
5. R / W............... The Captain Scott almost beat Amundsen to South Pole in 1912.
6. R / W............... Chicago is the main city on the Lake Michigan.
7. R / W............... The Amazon rainforests, said to be the lungs of the planet, are rapidly being cleared.
8. R / W............... You can see the Mount McKinley in the distance.
9. R / W............... What climber has not dreamt of climbing Everest?
10. R / W............... Turkey is surrounded by three of the world's most volatile regions: Middle East, Caucasus and Balkans

2. Complete the sentences using the right article.

1. ...... Austrian Alps are scenic but not exotic.
2. An estimated 15,000 people died in the eruption of ...... Mount Vesuvius that buried Pompeii in A.D. 79.
3. ...... London of the 18th century was very different from ...... London of today.
4. John Krakauer's novel has been a best-seller, reflecting a rising American fascination with the dark desert places of ...... Himalayas.
5. When Cartier discovered the mouth of ...... St Lawrence River in 1534, he found a thousand Basque vessels already fishing there. Eventually, the banks attracted fishermen from all over ...... Atlantic.
6. The President of ...... USA, Queen Elizabeth and the Heads of ...... European Union will hold a summit on the environment next month on ...... Isle of Wight.
7. In ...... Europe of tomorrow ...... France intends to set an example of a social model, striking a balance between state protection and freedom of action.
8. The thousands of American "snowbirds" who winter in ...... Arizona and drive their recreational vehicles north to ...... Alaska in summertime, spend little time in ...... Yukon on the way.
9. The 1,190 islands in ...... Maldives and ...... Marshall Islands are an average of only 3 meters above sea level.

Correction

1. **1**. the Atlantic - **2**. R - **3**. the West Indies - **4**. the Potomac - **5**. Captain Scott / the South Pole - **6**. Lake Michigan - **7**. R - **8**. Mount McKinley - **9**. R - **10**. the + Middle East / Caucasus / Balkans

2. **1**. The Austrian Alps - **2**. Mount Vesuvius - **3**. The London / the London - **4**. the Himalayas - **5**. the St Lawrence River / the Atlantic - **6**. the USA / the European Union / the Isle of Wight - **7**. the Europe / France - **8**. Arizona / Alaska / the Yukon - **9**. the Maldives / the Marshall Islands

74 ARTICLES A / AN / Ø

1. Spot the possible mistakes and correct them. Write R for Right.

1. R / W.............. He bought a umbrella at the local department store.
2. R / W.............. The average American eats three hamburgers the week.
3. R / W.............. In 2009, some 27 countries formed a union known as the EU.
4. R / W.............. An apple a day keeps a doctor away. (*Proverb*)
5. R / W.............. He smokes a pipe every evening before going to bed.
6. R / W.............. An university degree was one of the requirements for the position.
7. R / W.............. What an awful weather! When will rain ever stop?
8. R / W.............. Do you take a sugar in your coffee? Not any more, I'm on a diet now.
9. R / W.............. A FBI report showed that, for the eighth year in the row, violent crime in the United States declined sharply
10. R / W.............. He has headache. He works too hard.
11. R / W.............. The diabetes is an auto-immune disease.
12. R / W.............. The riot police were sent in to quell a riot that had broken out in local prison.

2. Complete the sentences using the right article.

1. My friend's parents were married in ..... Scottish chapel. **2**. Sally's been admitted to ..... hospital after an asthma attack. **3**. Mother is in ..... home. We just couldn't look after her any more. **4**. He doesn't like ..... work he does. It's dull. **5**. I like ..... market in your town. It's quaint. **6**. The Providence Express leaves from ..... platform 9. **7**. Many young people leave ..... school unable to read and write. **8**. ..... hospital is under threat of closure for financial reasons. **9**. What will you have for ..... breakfast? Nothing. I never eat ..... breakfast. **10**. ..... smallpox was eradicated 25 years ago. **11**. I'm planning on going on ..... holiday to New England. I'm all for ..... quiet, peaceful holiday. **12**. Even after ..... plague is eradicated, it may not be sensible to stop vaccinating against it. **13**. ..... Thanksgiving dinner is always an elaborate affair. **14**. ..... Church still plays a significant role in Great Britain, contrary to secular countries like France.

3. Complete the sentences using *at* / *in* or *to*.

1. The church I usually go ..... can seat over 2,000 people. **2**. I strongly recommend staying ..... the local hotel. **3**. ..... my home, we have dinner at 8. **4**. Her son wants to study economics ..... university. **5**. He's ..... home working on a new novel. **6**. She went ..... market to do some shopping.

Correction

1. 1. an umbrella (note : a + union / university / urinal, etc.) - **2**. a week - **3**. R - **4**. the doctor - **5**. his pipe - **6**. A university - **7**. ø awful weather (weather is uncountable here) / the rain - **8**. ø sugar (sugar is uncountable; a lump / a piece of sugar) - **9**. An FBI (watch how an f is pronounced in English) / a row - **10**. a headache (to have **a** headache) - **11**. Diabetes (no article with nouns of disease) - **12**. the local prison

2. **1**. a - **2**. ø - **3**. a - **4**. the - **5**. the - **6**. ø - **7**. ø - **8**. The - **9**. ø / ø - **10**. ø - **11**. ø / a - **12**. a - **13**. (A) - **14**. The

3. **1**. to - **2**. at / in - **3**. In - **4**. at - **5**. at - **6**. to

75 ARTICLES A / AN / Ø / THE

1. Spot the possible mistakes and correct them. Write R for Right.

1. R / W.............. Since Descartes, man has claimed he can dominate the nature, but the nature always gets her own back.
2. R / W.............. History of the world is only the opinion of the world.
3. R / W.............. The society imposes stereotypical roles on both sexes.
4. R / W.............. History only informs us what bad government is.
5. R / W.............. The weather routinely makes fools of forecasters.
6. R / W.............. Love is but the wisdom of the fool and the folly of the wise.
7. R / W.............. The music is the only sensual pleasure without vice.
8. R / W.............. A man is one who will give a woman anything except his seat on the streetcar.
9. R / W.............. Everyone is entitled to an education.
10. R / W.............. Walt Whitman's poem "When lilacs last in the door-yard bloom'd" mourned death of Abraham Lincoln.
11. R / W.............. To most of us real life is life we do not lead.
12. R / W.............. Some of the work you do at school will serve you for the rest of your lives.
13. R / W.............. Every religion believes that it has a monopoly on the truth.
14. R / W.............. America is society in which nearly everybody pays lip-service to the idea of equality of opportunity.

2. Complete the sentences using the right article.

1. The Constitution gave the Americans ...... democracy to "endure for generations". **2**. Scotland found herself richer for ...... oil and gas found off her coasts. **3**. Demand for ...... coal is concentrated in winter. **4**. ...... business of the Ford company is ...... business of America. **5**. Attitudes towards ...... capital punishment are the product of emotion, according to the defenders of ...... death penalty. **6**. In poor countries, irrigation accounts for 80% of water use, but most of ...... water just drains away. **7**. In America, despite the currency of ...... Spanish, ... English is the language for advancement. **8**. ...... rugby has become a means (as ...... cricket never did) for the Afrikaner to assert himself over the Englishman. **9**. ...... blues is a form that originated in New Orleans at the turn of the century. **10**. ...... air in Asia's cities, like ...... water in its rivers, contains levels of ...... dust and ...... smoke several times higher than in the rich countries' cities. **11**. You have to be ...... black to really play ...... jazz. **12**. An old friend of mine has just turned up out of ...... blue. I hadn't seen him for years.

Correction

1. **1**. nature / nature - **2**. The history (German proverb) - **3**. Society - **4**. R (Thomas Jefferson) - **5**. R - **6**. R - **7**. Music (Samuel Johnson) - **8**. Man - **9**. R - **10**. the death of Abraham Lincoln - **11**. the real life / the life (Oscar Wilde) - **12**. R - **13**. truth - **14**. a society

2. **1**. a - **2**. the - **3**. ø - **4**. The / the - **5**. ø / the - **6**. the - **7**. ø / ø - **8**. ø / ø - **9**. The - **10**. The / the / ø / ø - **11**. ø / ø - **12**. the

76 ARTICLES (REVIEW)

Circle the letter of the correct answer.

1. ... bear is in danger of becoming extinct.
a) A polar b) Polar c) The polar d) Any polar

2. I'm told he's not at ... office, but I know he is at ... work.
a) the / the b) ø / ø c) the / ø d) the / the

3. He taught me how to play ... violin.
a) the b) at the c) a d) ø

4. The Scots usually have ... porridge for ... breakfast.
a) ø / ø b) the / ø c) ø / a d) the / the

5. I can guess what you had for lunch, there is ... on your tie.
a) any egg b) an egg c) the egg d) egg

6. He works late at his office, yet he takes college courses three nights ... .
a) in every week b) per weekly c) in each week d) a week

7. The robbers were armed to ... teeth.
a) their b) ø c) the d) one's

8. He was wounded in ... chest during the ambush.
a) a b) the c) his d) ø

9. ... American cooking is not so bad as ... French say it is.
a) The / the b) the / ø c) ø / ø d) ø / the

10. The Marines showed ... great courage in the war.
a) a b) ø c) the d) any

11. ... in the kitchen. There's salted or unsalted.
a) The butter is b) A butter is c) Butters are d) The butters are

12. This is ... for anyone to buy!
a) a big lie too b) a too big lie c) too big a lie d) a lie too big

13. ... cell phone has become a highly fashionable item.
a) A b) The c) Ø d) One

14. If you want to go into business, you should take ... MBA.
a) a few b) ø c) an d) a

15. How much did ... crude oil cost in 1973?
a) any b) ø c) the d) a

16. Oysters are sold by ... dozen.
a) the b) one c) a d) ø

17. He's gone to ... and won't be back for a couple of hours.
a) restaurant b) cinema c) house d) church

18. He got caught traveling without ... ticket.
a) ø b) no c) one's d) a

Correction

1c ; animal species take article *the* : the + whale / the spotted owl / the deer, etc. - **2c** ; don't confuse the place and the abstract noun : the church = the building; to go to church = to practice one's religion - **3a** ; music instruments take *the* (play the piano / the cello / the guitar) although you can find "He plays drums in a local rock band." - **4a** ; no article for non-countable nouns and meals (to have lunch / dinner, etc.) - **5d** ; egg = the matter ÷ an egg - **6d** ; compare with a dime a dozen / ten cents a gallon, etc. - **7c** - **8b** ; external aggression, therefore article *the* (to be compared with : He broke his leg skiing) - **9d** ; cooking = a subject matter (compare : I love physics / math / economics) ; the French = adjective - **10b** ; courage = abstract noun - **11a** ; butter is mentioned in context - **12c** ; too stupid a mistake / too difficult an exercise, etc. - **13b** ; inventions take *the* article, except TV : the radar / the Internet / the wheel, etc. - **14c** - **15b** - **16a** - **17d** - **18d**

77 THIS / THAT

1. Spot the possible mistakes and correct them. Write R for Right.

1. R / W............... Do you understand what these paragraph means?
2. R / W............... You call that bravery? For me it's sheer cowardice.
3. R / W............... Come on, you can't be this stupid, surely!
4. R / W............... "How was the musical?" "Not all this good."
5. R / W............... I wonder what I'm doing in this city. I wanna go home!
6. R / W.............. The position of a lame-duck president is no more comfortable than this of an outgoing congress.
7. R / W............... What's that I hear about you wanting to become a nun?
8. R / W............... 2007 was an excellent year for Lehman Corp. This year, the stock shot up by 30 per cent.
9. R / W............... Have you heard from that Cornish girl you used to date?
10. R / W............... I've seen the remake of *Bill*. I didn't find it all this good.
11. R / W.............. No-one wants to take care of those dog of hers while she is away. It is so vicious.
12. R / W.............. What nutritionist are you talking about? Oh, you mean that? I thought you meant the one who wrote *The Ultimate Diet*.
13. R / W.............. The charms of this holiday resort that the middle classes used to flock to, are once again beginning to show.
14. R / W.............. Those days modern production methods require a better qualified and keener workforce.

2. Choose *this* or *that*. Tick the right box.

	This	*That*
1. Tell me about ... blonde you've met.		
2. The book has its weaknesses but it is a satisfying read for all		
3. Banks were making big money at ... time.		
4. Don't worry. ... shouldn't present too much of a problem.		
5. In ... country of ours, a great many road accidents are caused by badly-maintained vehicles.		
6. I told her there was nothing left to discuss and ... was		
7. The data released so far ... year look promising.		
8. I caught a bass that was ... long.		

Correction

1. **1**. this paragraph ; these = plural of this - **2**. R - **3**. that ; that = adverb - **4**. that - **5**. R - **6**. that - **7**. this - **8**. That ; reference to 2007 (past) ; this year = the current year - **9**. R - **10**. that - **11**. that ; those = plural of that ; *those dogs* would be acceptable - **12**. that one (= that nutritionist) - **13**. R - **14**. These ; the sentence is in the present tense

2. **This** : 4, 5, 7 - **That** : 1, 2, 3, 6, 8

78 QUANTIFIERS

1. Spot the possible mistakes and correct them. Write R for Right.

1. R / W............... Hurry up! There isn't plenty of time left.
2. R / W............... You use the phone too much at work.
3. R / W............... We needn't hurry. I have much time.
4. R / W............... Did it cost a lot to fix the car?
5. R / W............... Much people would choose to live next to a nuclear power station.
6. R / W............... Egypt recycles much of its Nile water.
7. R / W............... There is few hope of finding survivors.
8. R / W............... The EU has made few progress on fiscal harmonization.
9. R / W............... Scientists have little idea how many species exist in the first place.
10. R / W............... The rich world produces far too much children to keep up with its present population.
11. R / W............... Few years ago, they decided to outsource the production to India.

2. Circle the correct answer.

1. Brazil went through no fewer / less than three constitutions, in 1891, 1934 and 1946. **2**. Because of crime and violence, Washington is a place where fewer and fewer / less and less people want to live. **3**. "Never in the field of human conflict was so much / many owed by so much / many to so little / few." (Winston Churchill, August 20th, 1940). **4**. There seems few / little doubt that the assassination was carried out on orders from the Mafia. **5**. The Gulf War against Iraq in 1991 was swift, and allied casualties were less / few. **6**. Much / Many of the developing world has left Africa far behind.

3. Complete the sentences using the correct quantifier.

1. .... is known about the precise effects of the changing climate on fish stocks. **2**. We weren't given very .... information about their firm. **3**. Their salaries are incredibly low. Some of them earn as .... as $10,000 a year. **4**. .... countries are as mad about sport as South Africa. **5**. .... than half of her poems have been published so far. **6**. Meat is scarce, and shoppers queue to buy as .... as they can. **7**. .... museum art was acquired by dubious means, if not by outright looting. **8**. Better .... vision than none at all. **9**. .... thought .... of the inexperienced prime minister's chances when he was unexpectedly catapulted into power.

Correction

1. **1**. much time / a lot of time - **2**. R - **3**. plenty of / a lot of time / loads of time - **4**. R / much - **5**. Few - **6**. R - **7**. little - **8**. little - **9**. R - **10**. too few - **11**. A few

2. **1**. fewer - **2**. fewer and fewer - **3**. much / many / few - **4**. little - **5**. few - **6**. Much

3. **1**. Little - **2**. much - **3**. little - **4**. Few - **5**. Fewer - **6**. much - **7**. Much - **8**. a little - **9**. Few / much

79 COMPOUND ADJECTIVES

1. Find the antonyms and form compound adjectives.

1. well-behaved (boy)	
2. broad-minded	
3. run-down (district)	
4. fair-haired	
5. mass-produced	
6. hard-up (for money)	
7. flat shoes	
8. an old jalopy	
9. the rich	
10. recent (tradition)	

2. Find the compound adjective corresponding to each definition.

1. chosen among a list of many candidates ....

2. a disease you get from smoking ....

3. a plant paralyzed by a strike ....

4. a firm that loses money ....

5. a president that cannot be re-elected ....

6. a show where no more seats are available ....

3. Express the same idea using a compound adjective.

1. She has decided to wear a shirt with an open collar.

She has decided to wear an ....

2. He's about 45 years old.

He's a .... man.

3. He writes with his left hand.

He's ....

4. I'm going to sell these books to a bookstore which specializes in used books.

I'm going to sell these books to a ....

5. He kept a cool head throughout the race.

He remained .... throughout the race.

6. After the war, Great Britain underwent great changes.

.... Britain underwent great changes.

7. He has very bad eyes. He can't see very far.

He's ....

Correction

1. **1**. ill-behaved - **2**. narrow-minded - **3**. well-off - **4**. dark-haired - **5**. hand-made / tailor-made - **6**. well-off - **7**. high-heeled - **8**. a brand-new car - **9**. the have-nots - **10**. long-standing

2. **1**. hand-picked - **2**. a smoking-related disease - **3**. a strike-bound plant - **4**. a loss-making firm - **5**. a lame-duck president - **6**. a sold-out performance

3. **1**. an open-necked shirt - **2**. a middle-aged man - **3**. He's left-handed. **4**. a second-hand bookstore - **5**. cool-headed - **6**. post-war Britain - **7**. short-sighted

80 ADJECTIVES AND ADVERBS

1. Spot the possible mistakes and correct them. Write R for Right.

1. R / W............... The band played really good.
2. R / W............... I flew direct from Chicago.
3. R / W............... My motorcycle works fine, I've just had it tuned.
4. R / W............... They've bought a new car. So they're flatly broke.
5. R / W............... When I came home, the front door was widely open.
6. R / W............... She fell down and hurt herself badly.
7. R / W............... She looked angry at him.
8. R / W............... The number of dog-friendlily luxury hotels has doubled.
9. R / W............... Russia vows to restore friendly ties with neighbors.
10. R / W............... Brian came lately for the meeting.

2. Indicate whether the underlined words are adjectives or adverbs.

	Adj.	*Adv.*
1. I feel badly about it.		
2. She feels rather poorly today and prefers to stay at home.		
3. His breath smelled strongly of garlic.		
4. This is one of the most lively groups of pupils I've had in a long time.		
5. I had a friendly chat with my neighbor.		
6. The weapon was deadly. He was killed instantly.		
7. The cowardly soldier turned and fled instead of fighting.		

3. Complete the sentences using the appropriate adverbs or adjectives.

1. She keeps fit by training .... , at least twice .... **2**. She was breathing .... as if she had been running. **3**. She had been learning Russian for nine years and could speak it .... **4**. He's been working .... towards his master's degree. I'm sure he'll do .... **5**. She worked .... to pass her exams. She .... ever took any time off to rest. **6**. When he speaks English .... , I can understand everything he says. **7**. Shooting somebody in the back is .... **8.** He has been feeling .... since the death of his wife. He has no one to talk to. **9**. We .... escaped getting caught in flash floods while driving through Nevada.

Correction

1. **1**. well - **2**. R - **3**. R - **4**. flat - **5**. wide - **6**. R - **7**. angrily - **8**. dog-friendly - **9**. R - **10**. late

2. **Adv**. : 1, 3, 6 (instantly) - **Adj**. : 2, 4, 5, 6 (deadly), 7

3. **1**. regularly / weekly - **2**. hard - **3**. fluently - **4**. hard / well - **5**. hard / hardly - **6**. slowly - **7**. cowardly - **8**. lonely - **9**. narrowly

81 PARTICIPLES USED AS ADJECTIVES

1. Spot the possible mistakes and correct them. Write R for Right.

1. R / W............... Tarentino's last movie was amazed.
2. R / W............... She's always annoying about something.
3. R / W............... I met an interesting guy last week.
4. R / W............... The progress of medical research has been astonished.
5. R / W............... She was alone in the big house and terrifying.
6. R / W............... She was thrilled by her present.
7. R / W............... It is very frustrated when your computer is out of order.

2. Circle the correct answer.

1. The children are all exciting / excited because it's Christmas Eve.
2. I was very disappointed / disappointing with the actors.
3. Climbing to the top of Mount Everest had been exhausted / exhausting.
4. When they came back from their expedition, the mountaineers were so tired / tiring that they went straight to bed.
5. The old man was so confusing / confused he couldn't even recognize his own children.
6. The prime minister is worried / worrying about the financial situation.
7. The youngsters wandered aimlessly through the flat with bored / boring expressions on their faces.
8. She heard a frightened / frightening noise outside.
9. The terrifying / terrified incident unfolded, unbeknownst to the parents.

3. Complete the sentences using words from the list.

amazed / amazing / depressed / depressing / startled / startling / stunned / stunning / unexpected

1. It's .... that he should have escaped from the aircraft accident.
2. I was .... when I heard that he had rowed solo across the ocean.
3. We were .... by the gunshot.
4. News of his resignation was .... , to say the least.
5. His .... return after such a long absence surprised all of us. His showing up like that, out of the blue, was quite ....
6. The management was .... by the unions' refusal to negotiate. It was a .... blow to the company's traditional wage-bargaining policy.
7. The poet was much .... by the sunset. In turn, his .... poetry inspired many a young lover.
8. He felt terribly .... when he failed his driving test for the third time.
9. Cold, cloudy, rainy weather can be very ....

Correction

1. **1**. amazing - **2**. annoyed - **3**. R - **4**. astonishing - **5**. terrified - **6**. R - **7**. frustrating

2. **1**. excited - **2**. disappointed - **3**. exhausting - **4**. tired - **5**. confused - **6**. worried - **7**. bored - **8**. frightening - **9**. terrifying

3. **1**. amazing - **2**. amazed - **3**. startled - **4**. startling - **5**. unexpected / unexpected - **6**. stunned / stunning - **7**. inspired / inspiring - **8**. depressed - **9**. depressing

82 COMPARATIVES

1. Spot the mistakes and correct them. Write R for Right.

1. R / W............... Sending a letter takes longer than sending a fax.
2. R / W............... The economic forecasts weren't as rosier as announced.
3. R / W............... I prefer Cajun cooking to West Indian cooking: the former is as spicy than the latter.
4. R / W............... Using a computer is as easy than falling off a log.
5. R / W............... My flight arrived at the same time than yours.
6. R / W............... He has two daughters, the older is a student at Caltech.
7. R / W............... He is the eldest twin. He was born fifteen minutes before his brother.
8. R / W............... The teacher gave his students as much advice than he could before the exams.
9. R / W............... There is fewer traffic on the roads on a Monday morning than on a Sunday evening.
10. R / W............... During the first quarter, less companies went bankrupt than in the second.

2. Complete the sentences using the appropriate comparative form.

1. The house is too big. I'm going to move into a .... one next year.
2. The weather was quite warm. I had expected it to be ....
3. The party was quite noisy last night. I wish it had been ....
4. She is bored with her job. She hopes to find something ....
5. I hardly ever hear from her. I wish she wrote ....
6. The river is too deep here. We can't cross unless we find somewhere ....
7. The young are carefree about their future. I wish they were ....

3. Express opposite ideas using the comparative form of adjectives.

1. Surfing on the Internet is easier than most people think.
Surfing ....
2. She's better off than she was two years ago.
She ....
3. California grapes are cheaper than Chile grapes.
California grapes ....
4. It's closer than you think.
It's ....

Correction

1. **1**. R - **2**. as rosy as - **3**. less spicy than - **4**. as easy as - **5**. same + as - **6**. the elder - **7**. older - **8**. as much advice as - **9**. less traffic - **10**. fewer companies

2. **1**. smaller - **2**. cooler - **3**. quieter - **4**. more exciting - **5**. more often - **6**. shallower - **7**. more concerned

3. **1**. is harder than most people... - **2**. She's worse off than... - **3**. are more expensive than... - **4**. farther than...

83 SUPERLATIVES

1. Spot the possible mistakes and correct them. Write R for Right.

1. R / W............... It's one of the most picturesque village in the region.
2. R / W............... Namibia is one of the drier African countries I know.
3. R / W............... He turned out to be none the worst for his painful experience.
4. R / W............... The party didn't do the best at the polls than the President himself. Both were defeated.
5. R / W............... The longer you put off your visit to the dentist's, the worst it will be.
6. R / W............... The roads are dangerous this morning, all the most so as the area is shrouded in thick fog.
7. R / W............... We expected to pay thirty dollars but they charged us twice as most.
8. R / W............... Serena is the best player in the women's doubles team.
9. R / W............... Which of all those books did you like the better?

2. Complete the sentences using the superlative form of the adjectives in brackets.

1. In 1997, the Tories suffered their .... defeat since 1906. Tony Blair is the .... prime minister since 1812. (BAD) / YOUNG)
2. "The art of taxation," advised Louis XIV's treasurer, Jean-Baptiste Colbert, "consists in so plucking the goose to obtain the .... amount of feathers, with the .... possible amount of hissing." (LARGE / LITTLE)
3. Mexico City remains probably the world's .... big city, and border towns are sprawls of maquiladoras and sewage-filled rivers. (FILTHY)
4. In the past decade, wines from Chile have become the .... imports into the United States. (FAST-GROWING)

3. Circle the correct form (comparative or superlative).

1. A stronger / strongest euro will benefit the EU economy by helping to redistribute growth more evenly. **2**. Of the two sides, Brazil were the best / the better team but Argentina managed to win on penalties. **3**. The Republicans have pledged to cut income-tax rates farther / further than the Democrats. **4**. West Virginia is one of the less populated / the least populated states in the US. **5**. Three small children, the younger / the youngest aged four, were recently sent back to Nigeria without their parents.

Correction

1. **1**. villages - **2**. driest - **3**. none the worse - **4**. any better - **5**. the worse - **6**. all the more - **7**. twice as much - **8**. the better player - **9**. best

2. **1**. worst / youngest - **2**. largest / least - **3**. filthiest - **4**. fastest-growing

3. **1**. stronger - **2**. the better - **3**. further - **4**. the least populated - **5**. the youngest

84 SUCH / SO

1. Complete the sentences using *so, such* or *such a*.

1. The car was going ... fast that it missed the bend. **2**. Why make ...... fuss about what is only a detail, after all? **3**. The jury delivered its verdict with ...... passion that it seemed biased. **4**. The scale of World War II was ...... that it is hardly surprising that it continues to haunt us. **5**. Space is ...... vast that it might seem absurd to worry about its becoming cluttered. **6**. They had ...... fun that they promised themselves they'd be back. **7**. What motivates people to take ...... risks when going base-jumping? **8**. They had ...... heavy luggage they had to pay extra at the airport.

2. Combine the numbered and lettered elements to make a coherent sentence.

1. The lecture was so fascinating...
2. They live in such a distant suburb...
3. The financial crisis was so...
4. The firm had lost so much...
5. He was so...

a. ...... that they spend hours commuting each day.
b. ...... money it had to file under Chapter 11.
c. ...... that people stayed to the end.
d. ...... shocked he didn't say a word.
e. ...... serious that the White House ordered a general bail-out.

3. Combine the two sentences to form one using *such* or *so*.

1. The Smiths are tall people. Their heads almost touch the ceiling.
....

2. It is quite an expense. I can't afford it.
....

3. They're very nice. You immediately feel at home with them.
....

4. The FEMA tried to cope with four emergencies at once. The damage was widespread.
....

5. The city centre was polluted. Elderly people were requested to stay indoors. ....

6. Great strides have been made in medicine. Doctors will be able to cure some forms of cancer in the near future.
....

Correction

1. **1**. so - **2**. such a - **3**. such - **4**. such - **5**. so - **6**. such - **7**. such - **8**. such

2. 1c - 2a - 3e - 4b - 5d

3. **1**. The Smiths are such tall people that their heads almost touch the ceiling. **2**. The expense is such I can't afford it. **3**. They are so nice you immediately feel at home with them. **4**. The FEMA tried to cope with four emergencies at once, so widespread was the damage. **5**. The city centre was so polluted that elderly people were requested to stay indoors. **6**. Such great strides have been made in medicine that doctors will be able to cure some forms of cancer in the near future.

85 RELATIVE CLAUSES (SUBJECT RELATIVE PRONOUNS)

1. Spot the possible mistakes and correct them. Write R for Right.

1. R / W............... The theater, that burnt to the ground, has been rebuilt.
2. R / W............... The company which I work for is sending me to Brazil.
3. R / W............... All the papers I've read reported the same rumors.
4. R / W............... All what I need is a little peace and quiet.
5. R / W............... The first man which cycled the Darien Gap was I. Hibell.

2. Complete the sentences with *who, that, which* or ø.

1. The woman ...... lives opposite my house is a famous jazz singer. **2**. The poll, ... appeared in that magazine may not represent everyone. **3**. Distance is the cause ...... is most often responsible for ending a friendship. **4**. All ...... famous artists want is to be left alone. **5**. Everything ...... she told us was news to us. **6**. This is someone ...... spent most of his life in prison. **7**. Great Britain, ... is now an island, was once part of the European mainland. **8**. At half past five, ... was almost the end of the match, the score was 3-0. **9**. The parcel, ... he said he had sent me, never arrived. **10**. It's a plant ...... helps your digestion.

3. Combine the two sentences into one using a relative.

1. I bought a pineapple this morning. It is from Florida.

....

2. Intel is a well-known hi-tech company. It moved to Fort Worth in 1997.

....

3. Auster's *Brooklyn Follies* just came out. It is probably his best novel.

....

4. This watch is a Patek. My father gave it to me for my birthday.

....

5. She injured her right ankle while skiing. It is all right now.

....

6. The president made many promises during his campaign. He never kept them.

....

7. I missed the 9 A.M. flight to Denver. It is usually that flight I take to see my grand-children.

....

8. She's looking after the boss's children. They are spoilt little brats.

....

Correction

1. **1**. which - **2**. (that) - **3**. R - **4**. All I need - **5**. who

2. **1**. who / that - **2**. that / which - **3**. which / that - **4**. ø - **5**. that - **6**. who - **7**. which - **8**. which - **9**. which - **10**. that

3. **1**. The pineapple I bought this morning is from California. **2**. Intel, which is a well-known hi-tech company, moved to Fort Worth in 1997. **3**. Auster's *Brooklyn Follies*, which is probably his best novel, just came out. **4**. This watch, which my father gave me for my birthday, is a Patek. **5**. Her right ankle, which she injured while skiing, is all right now. **6**. The President, who made many promises during his campaign, never kept them. **7**. I missed the 9 A.M. flight I usually take to Denver to see my grand-children. **8**. She's looking after the boss's children, who are spoilt little brats.

86 RELATIVE CLAUSES (OBJECT RELATIVE PRONOUNS)

1. Circle the right relative.

1. Bull-fighting in Spain is which / what cricket is to the British or baseball to Americans: poetry, philosophy, pride. **2**. The Home Secretary is one of the few cabinet ministers which / whose political stock has undoubtedly gone up since the election. **3**. The president who / whom you were referring to yesterday and ø / who dropped the bomb on Japan, was Harry Truman. **4**. The science of genetics, in whose / which progress has been spectacular lately, is likely to shed light on many of life's secrets. **5**. We climbed to the top of the Washington Monument from what / which we had a beautiful view of the nation's federal capital

2. Complete the sentences using the right relative.

1. The castle, one wing of ...... has been rebuilt, has been reopened to the general public. **2**. By the time ...... you get to Phoenix, it will be 2 o'clock here. **3**. He has four children, the eldest of ...... is a lawyer and the youngest a physician. **4**. I remember vividly the day ...... I met her. **5**. I have two spare rooms upstairs, neither of ...... is occupied at the moment. **6**. The tourist wanted to know if I knew a place ...... they could get a decent meal at a decent price. **7**. Your problem, ... I have mulled over, is a tricky one.

3. Combine the two sentences into one using a relative.

1. Rumors tend to spread like wildfire. You shouldn't listen to them.

....

2. The tragedy unfolded at night. The parents weren't there.

....

3. There are 330m people around the world suffering from depression. 90 per cent of them won't get adequate treatment.

....

4. Her estate was worth several million pounds when she died. She left most of it to charity.

....

5. There were two flights out that night. I couldn't catch either.

....

6. The guy was short-sighted, deaf and a rotten driver. We were traveling in his car.

....

Correction

1. **1**. what - **2**. whose - **3**. whom / who - **4**. which - **5**. which

2. **1**. which - **2**. when - **3**. whom - **4**. when - **5**. which - **6**. where - **7**. which

3. **1**. Rumors, to which you shouldn't listen / which you shouldn't listen to, tend to spread like wildfire. **2**. The parents weren't there the night (when) the tragedy unfolded. **3**. There are 330m people around the world suffering from depression, 90 per cent of whom won't get adequate treatment. **4**. Her estate was worth several million pounds, most of which she left to charity. **5**. There were two flights out that night, neither of which I could catch. **6**. The guy, in whose car we were traveling, was short-sighted, deaf and a rotten driver.

87 RELATIVES (GENERAL)

1. Spot the mistakes and correct them. Write R for Right.

1. R / W............... She has two uncles, one of whose is a lawyer.
2. R / W............... The state in what I found him saddened me.
3. R / W............... The St Louis flight, that is due at 2 p.m., is late.
4. R / W............... Thomas Jefferson, that was George Washington's vice-president, was elected president in 1801.
5. R / W............... The British, many of which loved the Prince, went into mourning after her death.
6. R / W............... The woman who I was speaking to just now was my son's physics teacher.
7. R / W............... The LHC, which construction began a few years ago, intends to collide opposing beams of protons.
8. R / W............... John, most of whom family is Scottish, was brought up in Carlyle.

2. Circle the correct answer(s).

1. This is the largest plane that / ø I have ever seen. **2**. The drive-in, that / which is located outside town, is closed. **3**. The counselor, whose / which advice I had sought, was quite helpful. **4**. The burglars found nothing what / which was of any value. **5**. Which / What I don't like is the way she tries to ingratiate herself with the boss. **6**. She left early, what / which made me sad. **7**. He confessed to attacking two girls in March, one of who / whom died.

3. Write T (True) or F (False) for the statement that follows each numbered sentence.

1. My brother who runs an insurance company lives in Boston.
I have more than one brother : ......

2. My roommate, who is afraid of spiders, drives me nuts.
It is likely I have more than a roommate : ......

3. You can use the phone that is in my study.
I have one phone : ......

4. A car which has GPS is very convenient.
All cars have a GPS : ......

5. My watch, which worked yesterday, is giving me trouble again.
I have another watch I can use : ......

Correction

1. **1**. one of whom - **2**. in which - **3**. which - **4**. who - **5**. whom - **6**. whom - **7**. whose - **8**. most of whose

2. **1**. that *or* ø - **2**. which (there is only one) - **3**. whose - **4**. which - **5**. What - **6**. which - **7**. one of whom

3. 1T - 2F - 3F - 4F - 5F

88 POSITION OF ADVERBS

1. Spot the mistakes and correct them. Write R for Right.

1. R / W.............. He played the part of Lear beautifully in Peter Brooke's production last night in the new theatre.
2. R / W.............. Race in the US presidential campaign has become a very sensitive politically issue.
3. R / W.............. She is always asking me for money.
4. R / W.............. Young people nowadays are reluctant to go into apprenticeship.
5. R / W.............. He on average goes to the dentist's every year once.
6. R / W.............. He's been arrested often, but convicted never.
7. R / W.............. He refuses adamantly to go base-jumping with his colleagues.
8. R / W.............. They're going skiing on Sunday in the Rocky Mountains.
9. R / W.............. Negotiations were resumed officially between the two foes.
10. R / W.............. She usually saw her patients in the evening.

2. Put the adverbs in brackets in the correct position in the sentences.

1. I'll meet you. (AT TEN / OUTSIDE THE STATION / TOMORROW)
....
2. I go to Chile. (THREE TIMES / USUALLY / A YEAR)
....
3. She is embarrassed in front of the camera when she has to take her clothes off. (USUALLY) (SOMETIMES)
....
4. The police gathered all the evidence. (CAREFULLY)
....
5. The dressing-room was so packed that we had time to talk to the artist. (BARELY)
....
6. The frightened woman was trying to call 911. (DESPERATELY)
....
7. He's been drinking. (FOR YEARS / HEAVILY)
....
8. I never stay at the seaside, I have hated water. (LONG / ALWAYS)
....
9. The shareholders were impressed by the results of the company. (FAVORABLY)
....

Correction

1. **1**. in the new theatre last night - **2**. a very politically sensitive issue - **3**. R - **4**. Nowadays, young people are - **5**. On average, he goes... once every year - **6**. He's often been arrested... but never convicted - **7**. He adamantly refuses - **8**. They're going skiing in Colorado on Sunday - **9**. were officially resumed - **10**. R

2. **1**. I'll meet you outside the station at ten tomorrow. **2**. I usually go to Chile three times a year. **3**. She is sometimes embarrassed in front of the camera, usually when she has to take her clothes off. **4**. The police carefully gathered all the evidence. **5**. The dressing-room was so packed that we barely had time to talk to the artist. **6**. The frightened woman was desperately trying to call 911. **7**. He's been drinking heavily for years. **8**. I never stay long at the seaside, I have always hated water. **9**. The shareholders were favorably impressed by the results of the company.

89 THE CAUSATIVE

1. Spot the possible mistakes and correct them. Write R for Right.

1. R / W............... Unemployment benefits must be cut more drastically to have people look for work.
2. R / W............... The athletes, who had taken performance-enhancing drugs, made their medals and titles take away from them.
3. R / W............... The doctor had the patient's lungs X-rayed.
4. R / W............... The applicants were made fill in several forms.
5. R / W............... He had his suit clean at the dry-cleaner's.
6. R / W............... I managed to get her play a Schubert sonata.
7. R / W............... I had the store to deliver the washing machine Monday.
8. R / W............... Sally didn't want to go to her uncle's but her mother had her.

2. Write T (True) or F (False) for the statement that follows each numbered sentence.

1. I won't have you smoking in the house.
He is not allowed to smoke in the house : ......
2. I had my son make an appointment with the head teacher.
I am yet to meet the head teacher : ......
3. The PM got an adviser to write the speech for him.
The PM wrote the speech himself : ......
4. I'll have the car washed this week.
He'll wash the car himself : ......
5. Emma had her kitchen redone last Spring.
Emma didn't redo her kitchen herself : ......
6. Sophie got the charwoman to clean the flat before the guests arrived.
Sophie didn't do the house-cleaning : ......

3. Complete the sentence using *get, have, let* or *make* in the correct form.

1. You should .... a plumber to fix that leak. **2**. She always .... her paper corrected by her brother. **3**. As the two English youngsters didn't know any French, the old lady couldn't .... herself understood. **4**. TV is such a waste of time that Sarah won't .... her children watch it. **5**. Home owners .... their assessments lowered after the sub-prime crisis. **6**. As the house has been broken into repeatedly, I .... the police keep a eye on it this summer. **7**. The principal .... all the lockers searched for drugs. **8**. I can't .... you drive the car, you're not old enough.

Correction

1. **1**. make people look - **2**. had their medals and titles taken - **3**. R - **4**. were made to fill - **5**. He had his suit cleaned - **6**. to get her to play - **7**. I'll have the store deliver - **8**. made her

2. 1T - 2T - 3F - 4F - 5T - 6T

3. **1**. get - **2**. has - **3**. make - **4**. let - **5**. had - **6**. I'll have - **7**. had - **8**. let

90 INFINITIVES

1. Spot the possible mistakes and correct them. Write R for Right.

1. R / W............... Can you tell me where buy metro tickets?
2. R / W............... Listen to jazz music is relaxing.
3. R / W............... It is a real adventure travel across the Andes on foot.
4. R / W............... For the CEO to resign would do the firm great harm.
5. R / W............... Some grandparents find it a drag having look after their grand children.
6. R / W............... It would be foolish go on climbing in this fog.
7. R / W............... I'm wondering how get to the station with all this traffic.
8. R / W............... I can't afford to wait any longer.
9. R / W............... It was simply incredible for them have flown in a balloon round the world.

2. Circle the correct answer(s).

1. I'll have you to know / know that I'm very upset. **2**. For him to admit / admit that he had got it wrong was quite extraordinary. **3**. I've never known him to pay / pay for a drink. **4**. She doesn't let her children to play / play in the street. **5**. Not to increase / increase aid to flood-stricken countries would be criminal. **6**. Have the next candidate to come in / come in. **7**. All he did was to give / give us a lecture on civility. **8**. Why to bother / bother? It's all a waste of time. **9**. She was made to open / open her handbag at the entrance of the shop. **10**. Rather than to queue / queue for a bus, why not to take / take a cab? **11**. Can you tell me how to get / get to the station? **12**. Why not to invite / invite them for the week-end? **13**. I'm prepared to do anything but to work / work in finance. **14**. I'd like to lie down and to take / take a nap. **15**. How better to promote / promote an economically sensible reform than as an attempt to save / save the earth too?

3. Complete the sentences using the right verb in the correct form.

1. Visitors are asked not .... the animals. **2**. You seem .... on weight. **3**. My doctor has advised me .... up smoking. **4**. He seems to have disappeared, he is nowhere .... **5**. He's the only player .... 14 grand slam tournaments. **6**. .... children being used as slave-labor in the 21st century is a disgrace. **7**. He reminded me .... the television aerial before going off on vacation. **8**. E-mail allows us informally .... information. **9**. .... to classical music, you need a good hi-fi system and peace and quiet. **10**. At the police station, he was made .... a statement admitting his guilt.

Correction

1. **1**. where to buy - **2**. To listen to / Listening to - **3**. to travel - **4**. R - **5**. having to look - **6**. to go - **7**. how to get - **8**. R - **9**. to have flown

2. **1**. know - **2**. to admit - **3**. pay / to pay - **4**. play - **5**. to increase - **6**. come in - **7**. give / to give - **8**. bother - **9**. to open - **10**. queue / take - **11**. how to get - **12**. invite - **13**. work - **14**. take - **15**. to promote / to save

3. **1**. to feed - **2**. to have put on - **3**. to give - **4**. to be seen - **5**. to have won - **6**. To see - **7**. to unplug - **8**. to informally share - **9**. To listen - **10**. to sign

91 GERUNDS

1. **Write T (True) or F (False) for the statement that follows each numbered sentence.**

1. "When would you like to start?" "As soon as it stops raining."
They have already started : ......

2. I heard her sing at Carnegie Hall.
She's singing now : ......

3. I watched them playing chess for a while.
When I left, the game was still going on : ......

4. From here you can see the workers building the new stadium.
It has been built now : ......

5. I saw the lady cross the street
and reach the other side : ......

2. **Put the verbs in brackets in the correct form.**

1. The police started (fire) .... He felt a bullet (graze) .... his cheek. **2**. She can't stand (hear) .... the noise children make. **3**. We spotted a woodpecker (chip) .... away at the tree-trunk. **4**. I would have loved (go) .... to that concert. **5**. As the survivors sat (shiver) .... in the lifeboats, they watched the great ship (break) .... in two and (sink) .... **6**. Somebody was heard (prowl) .... around the house in the dead of night. **7**. What with income tax being so high, there is no point in (work) .... so hard. **8**. The undercurrent was so strong that the stranded surfboarder had difficulty (get) .... back to the beach. **9**. Although his first movies were worth (see) ...., his latest is probably one of his worst and not worth (go) .... to. **10**. Try (avoid) .... (be) .... late for once. **11**. Getting all the users and potential users of space to (contribute) .... to (clean) .... space up would be hard.

3. **Complete the sentences using the correct preposition.**

1. "I'm sorry ...... being late. It was good of you to wait for me." **2**. ...... entering the room, you could tell something fishy had been going on. **3**. Have you seen the mess in your room? How ...... tidying it up for a change? **4**. The Truman doctrine committed America ...... opposing the spread of communism. **5**. Bodyguards prevented us ...... approaching the president. **6**. The two lovebirds got married ...... their parents finding out. **7**. ...... carrying out the project, he gained the respect of his employer.

Correction

1. 1F - 2F - 3T - 4F - 5T

2. **1**. firing / graze - **2**. hearing - **3**. chipping - **4**. to go - **5**. shivering / break / sink - **6**. prowling - **7**. working - **8**. getting - **9**. seeing / going - **10**. to avoid / being - **11**. contribute / cleaning

3. **1**. for - **2**. On - **3**. about - **4**. to - **5**. from - **6**. without - **7**. In

92 INFINITIVES AND GERUNDS

1. Indicate whether the action has taken / is taking place (A) or not (B).

1. The kids denied breaking into the school during the long week-end. ......
2. Don't forget to write to your aunt. ......
3. I must remember to bring the keys with me. ......
4. He could remember talking to a stranger and then hearing the blast. ......
5. I regret to inform you that your application has been turned down by the admissions committee. ......
6. He decided to stop to have a smoke. ......
7. If you want to catch an early train it means getting up at six. ......
8. John will never forget seeing Miriam for the first time. ......
9. She didn't remember to water the plants. ......
10. Stop pulling my leg. ......
11. Would you mind not smoking? I'm trying to give up. ......

2. Circle the correct solution(s).

1. He was the first throwing / to throw his support behind the president.
2. We're considering to sell / selling the old flat in Queens.
3. She's decided retiring / to retire earlier.
4. Damn! I forgot to post / posting the parcel for Granny.
5. I can't remember to lock / locking the door on my way out.
6. He couldn't resist to buy / buying another iPod.
7. He stopped smoking / to smoke a cigarette in the shade.
8. He enjoys traveling / to travel alone.
9. They went on doing / to do their exam paper despite the noise.

3. Put the verbs in brackets in the infinitive or -ING form.

1. After doing a B.Sc. in France, his daughter went on (study) .... in the US. **2**. "Would you like (see) .... Ben Stiller's latest film tonight?" "Well, you know I don't like (go) .... out on Tuesday evenings." **3**. Our driver stopped (have) .... a pint at the pub on the way back. I had a cup of coffee. Actually I stopped (drink) .... beer ages ago. **4**. I had meant (buy) .... the Sunday papers but there was no newsagent's in the village. **5**. They don't allow (smoke) .... in the concert hall. They don't want (risk) .... (set) .... it on fire. **6**. The sound isn't very good. Have you tried (move) .... the aerial? **7**. Would you mind (pay) .... by check? We can't get the credit card machine (work) .... **8**. Once the president had finished (speak) .... the congressmen rose to their feet and gave him a standing ovation. The president then went on (shake) .... hands with the members.

Correction

1. 1A - 2B - 3B - 4A - 5A - 6B - 7B - 8A - 9A - 10A - 11A

2. **1**. to throw - **2**. selling - **3**. to retire - **4**. to post - **5**. locking - **6**. buying - **7**. to smoke - **8**. traveling - **9**. doing

3. 1. to study - **2**. to see / going - **3**. to have / drinking - **4**. to buy - **5**. smoking / to risk setting - **6**. moving - **7**. paying / to work - **8**. speaking / to shake

93 INFINITIVES AND GERUNDS (REVIEW)

Circle the letter of the right answer.

1. He denied ... that remark.
a) to have made b) to make c) making d) he has made

2. The old man did not remember ... to Chile as a child - it was too long ago.
a) to go b) go c) to be going d) going

3. Have you ever considered ... in Australia?
a) to live b) living c) to have lived d) live

4. ... too much of people and they end up getting irritable.
a) Ask b) To ask c) Asking d) Asked

5. It is no use ... . The decision is final.
a) to discuss b) arguing c) discussing d) to argue

6. The government seems determined ... swayed by the unions this time.
a) to not be b) of not being c) not to be d) to be not

7. The boy apologized and said he had not meant ... rude.
a) to be b) being c) having been d) to have been

8. Congress will need ... to implement all the new rules it has devised.
a) to reinforce b) reinforce c) of reinforcing d) reinforcing

9. Why not ... it before lunch?
a) doing b) to do c) having done d) do

10. Taking your time will help you rather than ... you.
a) to hinder b) hinder c) hindering d) it will hinder

11. That you love apples does not excuse ... my orchard!
a) you robbed b) you to rob c) your robbing d) your robbed

12. They spent the whole week-end ... .
a) packing b) in packing c) on packing d) at packing

13. She wondered why it hadn't occurred ... so.
a) her saying b) to say c) her to say d) to her to say

14. Your office really wants ... .
a) to clean b) cleaning c) us to clean d) being cleaned

15. The match will take place tomorrow, weather ... .
a) permits b) does it permit
c) permitting d) were it to permit

16. After more than 3 hours they succeeded ... the missing child.
a) to find b) in locating c) finding d) to locate

17. The principal ordered the boys ... .
a) stop to fight b) to stop to fight c) stop fighting d) to stop fighting

18. Any consensus will be a long time ... .
a) come b) coming c) to coming d) to come

Correction

1c - 2d - 3b - 4a - 5b - 6c - 7a - 8d - 9d - 10b - 11c - 12a - 13d - 14b - 15c - 16b - 17d - 18b

94 INDIRECT SPEECH

1. Spot the mistakes and correct them. Write R for Right.

1. R / W............... I don't know what is about the article.
2. R / W............... I haven't a clue who is that man over there.
3. R / W............... Can you tell me what time is it?
4. R / W............... We didn't know what was the speed limit in Virginia.
5. R / W............... Do you know how much is VAT on DVDs in England?
6. R / W............... George asked whether he was seeing us again soon.
7. R / W............... He asked why I don't get the job.
8. R / W............... She said she may drop by later.
9. R / W............... She asked does the job provides benefits.

2. Rewrite each sentence as indirect speech.

1. "I'm not sure if we'll see each other again," he said.
....

2. "Youth is the only time to have dreams," he remarked in a rare burst of romantic feeling.
....

3. "We'll meet again next summer," he promised.
....

4. "Do you think I should tell my parents about Cole?" she asked.
....

5. "How did you manage to put on so much weight at your aunt's?" my mother asked.
....

3. Use starters and turn the sentences into indirect speech.

1. When are we leaving?
She asked..

2. Where have you put my glasses?
He asked..

3. When is your holiday starting?
She wants to know..

4. Are you being attended to?
The salesgirl asked...

5. How do you like my recipe?
She asked..

Correction

1. **1**. I don't know what the article is about. **2**. I haven't a clue who that man over there is. **3**. Can you tell me what time it is? **4**. We didn't know what the speed limit was in Virginia. **5**. Do you know how much VAT is on DVDs in England? **6**. George asked whether he would be seeing us again soon. **7**. He asked why I didn't get the job. **8**. She said she might drop by. **9**. She asked if the job provided benefits.

2. **1**. He said that he wasn't sure they would ever see each other again. **2**. He remarked that youth was the only time to have dreams in a rare burst of romantic feeling. **3**. He promised we'd meet again next summer. **4**. She asked me if / whether I thought she should tell her parents about Cole. **5**. My mother asked me how I had managed to put on so much weight at my aunt's.

3. **1**. She asked when we were leaving. **2**. He asked where I had put his glasses. **3**. She wants to know when my holiday is starting. **4**. The salesgirl asked whether I was being attended to. **5**. She asked how I liked her recipe.

95 SUBORDINATING CONJUNCTIONS

1. Match the numbered elements with the lettered ones.

1. The unions will not resume negotiations ....
2. Some metals are malleable, ...
3. Much as I would like to help you with your math, ...
4. No matter what the environmentalists say, ...
5. Precautions are taken ....
6. She's been invited and would like to go to the party, ...
7. Traffic was all the more congested on the M6 ....
8. Although this car is very economical, ...
9. I have poor night vision, so I never drive after dark, ...
10. We came early, ...

a. production of genetically modified food will go ahead.
b. though whether her parents will let her go is another story.
c. unless I have to.
d. while others are so brittle that they break easily when bent.
e. as there had been a pile-up involving several vehicles.
f. so as to be sure of getting a good seat.
g. whenever a hurricane threatens to strike Florida.
h. unless the management offers major concessions.
i. I'm afraid I won't be able to. I have never had a head for figures.
j. you can't expect to get more than 50 miles to a gallon.

2. Complete the sentences using the correct conjunctions or prepositions.

1. .... cleaning his gun it went off accidentally. **2**. Hardly had the Panama Canal opened, in August 1914, ... Europe was plunged into war. **3**. .... it is growing stronger, the economy is not as vigorous as it should be. **4**. .... its selflessness, the Marshall Plan will always be linked with the hardening of the Cold War. **5**. .... much critics of Beijing's human rights record might disapprove of the deal, it will be signed. **6**. Start your career as soon as you can .... you'll be able to retire early. **7**. .... most of the family couldn't stand each other, the wedding was a very low-key affair. **8**. The most controversial of all American domestic policy issues, ... to permit abortion, was decided by the Supreme Court, and has continued to split opinion ever since. **9**. In November 1994, ... we forget, the Republican party resoundingly won control of Congress. **10**. .... had the talks begun than the unions decided to walk out. **11**. Poor countries recoil at the thought of UN reform, ... reform imposed by the Americans.

Correction

1. 1h - 2d - 3i - 4a - 5g - 6b - 7e - 8j - 9c - 10f

2. **1**. While - **2**. when - **3**. Even though - **4**. For all - **5**. However - **6**. so that - **7**. Since - **8**. whether - **9**. lest - **10**. No sooner - **11**. let alone

96 PHRASAL VERBS

Circle the letter of the correct answer.

1. In spite of promising to help us, Clara has ... of the project.
a) backed out b) given up c) taken back d) turned his back

2. The official told me he would look ... my complaint.
a) through b) into c) down on d) out for

3. "When does the Art College break ...?" "On June 30th."
a) off b) down c) through d) up

4. I'm afraid I have to go ... my promise to lend you $10,000.
a) in for b) out of c) back on d) away from

5. They are fed up and would like to get ... .
a) it over with b) over with it c) over it with d) with it over

6. After their quarrel Jane and William made ... .
a) up with b) over c) along d) up

7. Don't ring ..., I haven't finished my story yet.
a) out b) down c) off d) away

8. Fill ... the data requested on the form.
a) upon b) in c) over d) around

9. The man sitting opposite me turned ... to be a friend of my brother's.
a) up b) in c) on d) out

10. We don't want to strike, but we'll certainly walk ... if we have to.
a) down b) over c) out d) in

11. If we want to buy a house, we'll have to ... our spending.
a) care of b) cut back on c) let down d) miss out

12. You must give me some time to think ... .
a) it about b) to it c) through it d) it over

13. .We had to put ... our trip to Italy until Easter.
a) off b) down c) out d) in

14. Owing to the recession money is hard to come ... .
a) to b) by c) into d) out

15. Despite lengthy negotiations, the talks between the two countries ... .
a) broke away b) gave up c) broke down d) gave out

16. I feel much fitter since I ... swimming.
a) broke off b) took up c) set about d) made up

17. My request for sabbatical leave was ... .
a) turned down b) put down c) broken off d) set off

18. She brought ... her children on her own after he husband died.
a) in b) down c) up d) off

Correction

1a - 2b - 3d - 4c - 5a - 6d - 7c - 8b - 9d - 10c - 11b - 12d - 13a - 14b - 15c - 16b - 17a - 18c

97 IRREGULAR VERBS

Circle the letter of the right answer.

1. Did you ... today's papers?
a) read b) rode c) ridden

2. I'd rather you ... more attention in class.
a) pay b) payed c) paid

3. Carver ... *Cathedral*, probably his best collection of stories.
a) has writen b) writed c) wrote

4. I'm soaking wet. I wish I ... my umbrella.
a) didn't forget b) had taken c) had forgotten

5. Innovative work methods have been introduced since he ... CEO.
a) became b) becamed c) becomes

6. The lights are still on. They ... to turn them off.
a) forget b) forgot c) forgotten

7. The information he ... turned out to be reliable.
a) gave b) has given c) had given

8. The price of crude ... sharply yesterday.
a) risen b) rised c) rose

9. He ... the shuttle to London. Should be here any minute.
a) catched b) caught c) has catched

10. In the 2000s, the country was ... by a food crisis.
a) stricken b) stroked c) struck

11. He's ... me $10,000 I'm supposed to pay back next year.
a) lent b) lended c) loans

12. Alaska's ... oil reserves could last 100 years.
a) proof b) proved c) proven

13. As they were cold and shivering, they ... a fire around which they ... .
a) light/kneeled b) lit/knelt c) lighted/knell

14. I ... smoking years ago.
a) quited b) quit c) quitten

15. He ... finest carpets, some so intricate that he could pack in 964 knots of thread in a square inch of the yarn.
a) weaved b) waved c) wove

16. He did not choose to be ... into the national and international spotlight.
a) flung b) flang c) flingen

17. He ... a major shock by coming from a set down to beat the world's number one and title holder.
a) sprang b) sprung c) springed

18. Have you ever ... a horse?
a) rided b) ridden c) rode

Correction

1a - 2c - 3c - 4b - 5a - 6b - 7a - 8c - 9b - 10c - 11a - 12c - 13b - 14b - 15c - 16a - 17b - 18b

IRREGULAR VERBS

- **Infinitive and past participle are identical.**

become	became	become	*devenir*
come	came	come	*venir*
run	ran	run	*courir*

- **Past and past participle are identical.**

behold	beheld	beheld	*contempler*
bend	bent	bent	*se pencher, courber*
beseech	besought	besought	*supplier*
bid	bid/bade	bid/bade/bidden	*ordonner, enchérir*
bind	bound	bound	*lier*
bleed	bled	bled	*saigner*
bring	brought	brought	*apporter*
build	built	built	*construire*
burn	burnt/burned	burnt/burned	*brûler*
burst	burst	burst	*éclater*
buy	bought	bought	*acheter*
catch	caught	caught	*attraper*
cling	clung	clung	*s'accrocher*
creep	crept	crept	*ramper*
deal	dealt	dealt	*traiter, négocier, distribuer*
dig	dug	dug	*creuser*
dream	dreamt/dreamed	dreamt/dreamed	*rêver*
earn	earnt/earned	earnt/earned	*gagner*
feed	fed	fed	*(se) nourrir*
feel	felt	felt	*sentir, éprouver*
fight	fought	fought	*se battre, combattre*
find	found	found	*trouver*
flee	fled	fled	*fuir, s'enfuir*
fling	flung	flung	*lancer*
get	got	got	*obtenir*
grind	ground	ground	*moudre*
hang	hung	hung	*pendre, suspendre*
hear	heard	heard	*entendre*
hold	held	held	*tenir*
keep	kept	kept	*garder, conserver*
kneel	knelt	knelt	*s'agenouiller*
lay	laid	laid	*poser, étendre*

lead	led	led	*mener, conduire*
leap	leapt	leapt	*bondir*
learn	learnt/learned	learnt/learned	*apprendre*
leave	left	left	*laisser, quitter*
lend	lent	lent	*prêter*
light	lit	lit	*allumer, éclairer*
lose	lost	lost	*perdre*
make	made	made	*faire*
mean	meant	meant	*signifier*
meet	met	met	*rencontrer*
pay	paid	paid	*payer*
say	said	said	*dire*
seek	sought	sought	*chercher*
sell	sold	sold	*vendre*
send	sent	sent	*envoyer*
shine	shone	shone	*briller*
shoot	shot	shot	*tirer*
sit	sat	sat	*être assis*
sleep	slept	slept	*dormir*
slide	slid	slid	*glisser*
smell	smelt/smelled	smelt/smelled	*sentir*
speed	sped	sped	*foncer*
spell	spelt	spelt	*épeler*
spend	spent	spent	*dépenser*
spill	spilt	spilt	*verser*
spin	spun/span	spun	*filer, pivoter*
spit	spat	spat	*cracher*
stand	stood	stood	*être debout, se tenir*
stick	stuck	stuck	*coller*
sting	stung	stung	*piquer*
strike	struck	struck	*frapper*
swing	swung	swung	*balancer*
sweep	swept	swept	*balayer*
teach	taught	taught	*enseigner*
tell	told	told	*raconter*
think	thought	thought	*penser*
understand	understood	understood	*comprendre*
weep	wept	wept	*pleurer*
win	won	won	*gagner*
wind	wound	wound	*enrouler, remonter*
wring	wrung	wrung	*tordre*

- **The three forms are different.**

be	was/were	been	*être*

begin	began	begun	*commencer*
bite	bit	bitten	*mordre*
drink	drank	drunk	*boire*
go	went	gone	*aller*
grow	grew	grown	*grandir, faire pousser*
know	knew	known	*savoir, connaître*
lie	lay	lain	*être couché*
ride	rode	ridden	*aller à cheval / en voiture, circuler*
ring	rang	rung	*sonner*
show	showed	shown	*montrer*
shrink	shrank	shrunk	*rétrécir*
sing	sang	sung	*chanter*
sink	sank	sunk	*couler*
spring	sprang	sprung	*jaillir*
stink	stank	stunk	*puer*
swim	swam	swum	*nager*

• **The three forms are identical.**

beset	beset	beset	*assaillir*
bet	bet	bet	*parier*
burst	burst	burst	*éclater*
cast	cast	cast	*jeter*
cost	cost	cost	*coûter*
fit	fit	fit	*aller, correspondre*
hit	hit	hit	*frapper*
hurt	hurt	hurt	*blesser, faire mal*
let	let	let	*laisser, permettre*
put	put	put	*poser, mettre*
quit	quit	quit	*abandonner*
read	read	read	*lire*
set	set	set	*placer, sertir, établir*
shed	shed	shed	*verser (larmes), perdre (feuilles)*
shut	shut	shut	*fermer*
split	split	split	*fendre*
spread	spread	spread	*répandre*
thrust	thrust	thrust	*fourrer, enfoncer*
upset	upset	upset	*bouleverser*

• **Past with *-a, -o, -i, -e* and past participle with *-en/n*.**

arise	arose	arisen	*s'élever*
awake	awoke	awoken	*s'éveiller*

blow	blew	blown	*souffler*
break	broke	broken	*briser*
chide	chid	chidden	*gronder*
choose	chose	chosen	*choisir*
draw	drew	drawn	*dessiner*
drive	drove	driven	*conduire*
eat	ate	eaten	*manger*
fall	fell	fallen	*tomber*
fly	flew	flown	*voler*
forbid	forbade	forbidden	*interdire*
forget	forgot	forgotten	*oublier*
forgive	forgave	forgiven	*pardonner*
freeze	froze	frozen	*geler*
give	gave	given	*donner*
hide	hid	hidden	*cacher*
rise	rose	risen	*augmenter*
see	saw	seen	*voir*
sew	sewed	sewn	*coudre*
shake	shook	shaken	*secouer*
steal	stole	stolen	*dérober*
swear	swore	sworn	*jurer*
take	took	taken	*prendre*
tear	tore	torn	*déchirer*
throw	threw	thrown	*jeter, lancer*
wake	woke	woken	*s'éveiller*
wear	wore	worn	*porter (sur soi)*
weave	wove	woven	*tisser*
withdraw	withdrew	withdrawn	*se retirer*
write	wrote	written	*écrire*

SOME COMMON PHRASAL VERBS

Phrasal verbs	**Meaning**
ask sb **round**	invite to one's home
blow sth **out**	stop burning by blowing
blow sth **up**	fill with air, water, make explode
break down	stop functioning
bring sth **about**	make sth happen
bring sth **out**	introduce (a new product)
bring sb **up**	raise (children)
burn (sth) **down**	burn completely
call sb **back**	return a phone call
call off	cancel

call sb **up**	telephone sb
carry on	continue
carry sth **out**	pursue a plan
catch on	become popular
cheer sb **up**	make sb feel happier
clean sth **up**	clean sth completely
clear up	make clear
come about	happen
come along	accompany
come off	become detached
come out	appear
come up	arise
come up with sth	invent
cover sth **up**	cover completely, conceal
cross sth **out**	draw a line through
cut sth **down**	bring down by cutting
cut sth **off**	stop supplying, remove by cutting
cut sth **out**	remove by cutting
dream sth **up**	invent
dress up	put on special or formal clothes
drink sth **up**	drink completely
drop by / in	visit unexpectedly
drop sb / sth **off**	take sb/sth to a place and leave them/it there
drop out (of sth)	leave
eat out	eat in a restaurant
end up	do sth unexpected or unintended, reach a final destination or place
fall off	become detached
figure sth / sb **out**	understand (after thinking about)
fill sb / sth **in**	complete with information (form, application)
find sth **out**	learn information
follow sth **through**	complete
fool around	be playful
get sth **across**	get people to understand an idea
get ahead	make progress, succeed
get along (with)	be on good terms (with)
get back	return
get by	survive
get sth **out** of sth	benefit from
get together	meet
get up	rise from bed

give sth **away**	give without charging money
give sth **up**	abandon, stop
go after sb / sth	pursue
go along (with)	act in agreement (with)
go off	explode (gun, fireworks)
go on (+ ING)	continue (to)
go up	be built
hand sth **in**	give some work to sb
hand sth **out**	distribute
hang up	put the phone down
hang sth **up**	put on a hanger / a hook
help sb **out**	assist
hold on	wait, not hang up (the phone)
keep (sb / sth) **away**	(cause to) stay at a distance
keep on (+ ING)	continue (to)
keep sth **on**	not remove (clothes, jewelry)
keep up (with sb)	go as fast as
lay sb **off**	terminate sb's employment
leave sth **on**	not turn off (light, radio), not remove (clothes, jewelry)
leave sth **out**	omit
let sb **down**	disappoint
let sb / sth **in / out**	allow to enter / to leave
light (sth) **up**	illuminate
look out	be careful
look sb / sth **over**	examine
look sth **up**	try to find (in a book / on the Internet)
make sth **up**	invent
pass sth **round**	distribute
pay sth **back**	repay
pay off	be worthwhile
pick sb / sth **out**	select, identify
pick up	improve
pick sb / sth **up**	lift, get an idea
play around	have fun
point sb / sth **out**	indicate
put sth **away**	put in an appropriate place
put sth **back**	put in its original place
put sb / sth **down** (to)	stop holding, attribute (to)
put sth **off**	postpone
put sth **on**	get dressed (clothing)
put (sth) **together**	assemble
put (sth) **up**	erect

run into sb	meet sb unexpectedly
run out (of sth)	not have enough of a supply
see sth **through**	complete
set sth **off**	cause to explode
set sth **up**	establish (firm), prepare for use
show sb / sth **off**	display the best features
show up	appear
sign up	register
stay up	remain awake
stick with / to (sb / sth)	not give up
straighten up	make neat
switch on	start (machine)
take sth **away / off**	remove
take sb **on**	hire, employ
take sth **out**	borrow (a book from a library)
talk sb **into**	persuade
talk sth **over**	discuss
team up with sb	start to work with
tear sth **down**	destroy
tear sth **up**	tear into small pieces
think sth **over**	consider
think sth **up**	invent
throw away / out	discard
try sth **on**	put clothing on to see if it fits
try sth **out**	find out if sth works
turn sb / sth **down**	reject, decrease the volume (radio)
turn sb / sth **into**	transform
turn sth **off**	stop (a machine)
turn sth **on**	start (a machine)
turn out	have a particular result
use sth **up**	consume completely
watch out	be careful
work sth **off**	remove by work or activity
work out	resolve, exercise
work sth **out**	solve
write sth **down**	write on a piece of paper
write sth **up**	write in a finished form

Dans la série ***Bloc-notes***

Allemand

- ***24 heures pour réussir l'écrit*** [niveau 2]
- ***Los!*** *Petits exercices de grammaire allemande pour bien réviser* [niveau 1]
- ***Lustig!*** *Apprendre et réviser son vocabulaire allemand en s'amusant* [niveau 1]
- ***SOS allemand.*** *Révision systématique de la grammaire et du vocabulaire* [niveau 1] & [niveau 2]
- ***Starten!*** *Communiquer efficacement en allemand* [niveau 2]
- ***Endlich!*** *Mieux comprendre l'Allemagne* [niveau 2]
- ***Tester sa grammaire allemande*** *en 12 séances et 1001 questions-réponses* [niveau 2]
- ***Ab die Post!*** *Apprendre et réviser les préverbes allemands en s'amusant*
- ***Ende gut, alles gut!*** [grands débutants]

Arabe

- ***Je parle arabe*** [niveau 1]
- ***Takallam.*** *Communiquer efficacement en arabe*

Chinois

- ***Zhēn bàng!*** *Parler chinois* [niveau 2]
- ***Tang hulu.*** *Friandises pour goûter la saveur des mots en chinois* [niveau 1]

Espagnol

- ***¡Así!*** *Apprendre ou réviser les bases de la grammaire espagnole en s'amusant* [niveau 1]
- ***Réussir son BTS espagnol*** [niveau 2]
- ***¡Vocabulario!*** *Apprendre et réviser son vocabulaire en jouant* [niveau 1]
- ***¿Sé o Sepa?*** *Apprendre et réviser les bases de la conjugaison espagnole en s'amusant* [niveau 1]
- ***¡Sin falta!*** L'espagnol sans faute. Jeux d'orthographe

FLE

- ***Ouf !*** *apprendre et réviser le vocabulaire français en s'amusant* [niveau 1]

Hébreu

- ***Milim.*** *Apprendre et réviser le vocabulaire hébraïque en s'amusant* [niveau 1]

Italien

- ***Giochi e parole.*** *Apprendre et réviser le vocabulaire italien en s'amusant* [niveau 1] & [niveau 2]
- ***Pronto ? Pronti !*** *Grammaire et vocabulaire pour débutants* [niveau 1]
- ***Prove.*** *Testez votre niveau en italien* [niveau 1] & [niveau 2]

Japonais

- ***Kakikata.*** *Écrire en japonais* [niveau 1]
- ***Mikado.*** *Apprendre ou réviser le vocabulaire japonais de base en s'amusant* [niveau 1]
- ***Tsukemono.*** *Pickles pour relever la saveur les mots en japonais* [niveau 1]

Occitan

- ***Òsca !*** *Je parle occitan* [niveau 1]

Roumain

- ***Drum bun.*** *Apprendre et réviser son vocabulaire roumain en s'amusant* [niveau 1]

Russe

- ***Je parle russe !*** *Grammaire pour débutants* [niveau 1] & [niveau 2]
- ***Zakouski.*** *Les amuse-bouche de l'alphabet cyrillique* [niveau 1]
- ***Granitsa.*** *Communiquer efficacement en russe* [niveau 2]

Achevé d'imprimer en septembre 2010 par Normandie Roto Impression s.a.s., 61250 Lonrai
N° d'impression : 103055 - Dépôt légal : septembre 2010 - Imprimé en France